NUCLEAR SECURITY

Other Books in the At Issue Series:

NUCLEAR SECURITY

Helen Cothran, *Book Editor*

David L. Bender, *Publisher*
Bruno Leone, *Executive Editor*

Bonnie Szumski, *Editorial Director*
Stuart Miller, *Managing Editor*

An Opposing Viewpoints® Series

Greenhaven Press, Inc.
San Diego, California

Library of Congress Cataloging-in-Publication Data

Nuclear security / Helen Cothran, book editor.
       p.   cm. — (At issue)
    Includes bibliographical references and index.
    ISBN 0-7377-0477-2 (pbk. : alk. paper) —
ISBN 0-7377-0478-0 (lib.)
    1. Nuclear weapons. 2. Nuclear arms control. 3. United States—
Military policy. 4. World politics—1989–   I. Cothran, Helen.
II. At issue (San Diego, Calif.)

U264 .N81624   2001
355.02'17—dc21   00-030904
                                                                    CIP

©2001 by Greenhaven Press, Inc., PO Box 289009,
San Diego, CA 92198-9009

Printed in the U.S.A.

Every effort has been made to trace owners of copyrighted material.

Table of Contents

Introduction

In August 1945, the United States dropped atomic bombs on the Japanese cities of Hiroshima and Nagasaki, bringing World War II to a close. Some 140,000 people died in the blasts, and many thousands died later from radiation sickness. The bombing of Hiroshima was the first use of atomic weapons, and the detonation set off a decades-long nuclear arms race between the former Soviet Union and the United States. The Cold War—as that arms race is called—cost both countries billions of dollars, created a global atmosphere of fear and mistrust, and eventually precipitated the collapse of the Soviet Union. With the dissolution of the Soviet Union in 1990, the Cold War ended, and so did much of the public's concern about nuclear weapons.

However, nuclear security is an even greater concern today than it was during the Cold War. The nuclear arms race during the Cold War was marked by caution and restraint and was played out by participants with an ocean between them. By contrast, nuclear proliferation today is characterized by unstable regional conflicts, lack of effective intelligence systems that could prevent an accidental deployment, and far more players, some of whom may not be deterred by fear of nuclear retaliation. Until recently, only five countries—the United States, Russia, England, France, and China—possessed nuclear capabilities. However, in 1998, India and Pakistan—contentious neighbors with a history of war—detonated nuclear bombs. Israel is purported to have nuclear weapons without declaring them. Furthermore, rogue nations—countries such as Iraq and Iran that the United States fears because they act outside the bounds of international law—have been acquiring nuclear technology from China and North Korea. A portion of this technology originates in the former Soviet Union, which has experienced nuclear security problems since its dissolution. Many of its nuclear sites remain unguarded, and the numerous institutional safeguards that once curtailed the proliferation of nuclear technology are now weakened.

As nuclear security becomes increasingly threatened, calls for more nuclear arms as well as calls for disarmament grow more vociferous. Many opponents of nuclear arms believe that the inherent risk of nuclear weapons—global annihilation—make the possession and use of these weapons immoral and indefensible. They assert that if countries persist in maintaining nuclear arsenals as a defense against growing nuclear threats, the world will actually be less safe. Nations that maintain a nuclear arsenal encourage others to develop nuclear weapons as a defense, abolitionists argue, which increases the likelihood that a mistaken or intentional deployment somewhere in the world will set off a sequence of retaliatory deployments that could eventually destroy the earth. The Goodpaster Committee for the Project on Eliminating

Weapons of Mass Destruction asserts that "only [an international] policy aimed at steadily curbing global reliance on nuclear weapons . . . is likely to progressively eliminate nuclear dangers."

U.S. abolitionists argue that eradicating nuclear weapons is in the best interest of the United States. Jonathon Schell, author of the 1981 book *The Fate of the Earth*, which was hailed as the definitive warning of nuclear peril, argues that the only serious threat the United States faces is from nuclear arms. Therefore, he contends, "the U.S. more than any other country probably has the most to gain from the global abolition of nuclear weapons." Most U.S. abolitionists support international nuclear arms control agreements such as the Comprehensive Test Ban Treaty, which prohibits the testing of nuclear weapons. Only by restraining nations from developing nuclear weapons by force of international law, they contend, can proliferation be stopped.

Other people believe that the goal of nuclear disarmament, however noble, is simply unrealistic. Since the technology to build nuclear weapons has been invented and cannot be un-invented, they argue, rogue countries will always be able to obtain the know-how and materials to make atomic bombs. The only way for the United States to combat nuclear threats from these countries is to possess greater nuclear firepower, they contend. Proponents of nuclear weapons argue that nuclear arsenals have actually made the world safer by raising the stakes of warfare. Whereas wars waged with conventional weapons can be won and are therefore viewed as profitable, nuclear war is unwinnable—since it would guarantee the destruction of both parties—and is therefore unlikely to be waged. The result is less warfare and more international stability, supporters of nuclear arms maintain. Richard N. Haass, director of foreign policy studies at the Brookings Institute, contends that "the cold war only remained cold because both the United States and the Soviet Union understood that any direct confrontation between them would likely escalate into a nuclear holocaust."

Proponents of nuclear arms are also wary of international treaties designed to abolish nuclear weapons. Treaties such as the 1968 Nuclear Non-Proliferation Treaty, which prohibited nations without nuclear weapons from obtaining them, and the 1996 Comprehensive Test Ban Treaty, which called for a ban on all testing of nuclear weapons, have been ineffective at stopping proliferation, they contend. The *Wall Street Journal* claims that "there is ample evidence that arms-control agreements have done more to spread arms than to suppress them." Nuclear arms proponents assert that some treaty signatories, such as the United States, abide by such treaties while other countries, such as China, cheat and continue to develop their nuclear arsenals.

As nuclear security becomes increasingly imperiled due to the proliferation of nuclear arms, scientists, military leaders, and concerned organizations worldwide have voiced differing views on how to contain the threat. The threat of nuclear disaster is greater today because of the increasing number of nations who possess nuclear technology, but also because nuclear weapons are now more deadly than ever. Since the United States' Manhattan Project developed the atomic bomb in 1945, advanced technology has made nuclear weapons more destructive. The weapons used in Japan in 1945 produced energy equivalent to about

20,000 tons of TNT; today's thermonuclear bombs generate energy equivalent to many millions of tons of TNT.

The splitting of plutonium and uranium atoms in the New Mexico desert decades ago ushered in one of the most momentous debates in history. The question of how to contain the dangers posed by nuclear weapons is the focus of *At Issue: Nuclear Security*.

1

Nuclear Security:
An Overview

John Beckham

John Beckham is a staff writer for the Los Angeles Times, *a daily news-paper serving the greater Los Angeles area.*

The doomsday clock—created in 1947 at the University of Chicago—represents the changing state of nuclear security around the world. Scientists, arms experts, and political scientists move the hands of the clock forward or back as they see the threat of nuclear disaster—represented by midnight—increase or decrease. For the most recent update in 1996, they determined that the world was in greater danger of nuclear disaster than it had been in 1991 and set the hands of the clock closer to midnight. A destabilized Russia, regional conflicts in the Middle East and Asia, and the nuclear ambitions of North Korea and Iraq have increased the world's nuclear danger, they asserted. Not everyone on the board was pessimistic about the status of nuclear security, however; optimists view nuclear bombs as a way to keep peace, not destroy it.

Humans first harnessed the atom at the University of Chicago in 1942. On the campus, a Henry Moore sculpture pays homage to that storied chain reaction.

In an auditorium a short walk away, another symbol of the Nuclear Age recently sat center stage. It was time again to set the Doomsday Clock.

Since it first appeared on the cover of the *Bulletin of Atomic Scientists* in 1947, the clock has reflected the state of international security (with midnight marking nuclear disaster). Set originally at 11:53, the clock has moved forward and back over the years.

Since 1991, the time has sat at 11:43. In December 1996, a handful of nuclear physicists, political scientists, former bomb designers and arms experts held the first public debate on where to move the clock's hands.

Some had reasoned that with the collapse of the Soviet Union and a perceived easing of worldwide tensions, the experts would turn back the clock further. Instead,they concluded that the world has grown more dangerous over the past four years and that the risk of an atomic weapon detonating somewhere on Earth has grown.

They have reset the time at 11:46, 14 minutes before nuclear midnight.

The cheerful 1991 assessment—the most optimistic in the clock's 48-year history—was based on the end of the Cold War, downsizing of superpower nuclear arsenals, the end of proliferation and reductions in nuclear waste.

The world is increasingly dangerous

But that promise was not borne out, a panel of 12 told the 18 members of the Board of the *Bulletin of Atomic Scientists.*

The testimony touched on nihilistic terrorists, unratified chemical and biological treaties, a growing rich-poor gap, rogue nations, chaos in Russia, and a world awash in legitimate and black market plutonium and warheads.

According to the experts, the world was not only a brutish place but one in which life was as solitary, poor and short as it had been for centuries.

The collapse of the Soviet Union, celebrated in 1991, actually has contributed to the growing specter of atomic detonations, according to the testimony. The Russian military, "disoriented, weakened and humiliated, could become a serious obstacle to stability," said Igor Khripunov, who negotiated for the Soviets during arms talks.

The disarmament treaties have become hollow victories, he added. The Russians cannot afford to comply with the existing treaties, and there is little money to destroy chemical weapons. Shaky finances also make the sale of centrifuges, reactors and perhaps warheads very tempting, said author and investigator David Albright.

Regional troubles in the Middle East and Asia, witnesses warned, have led to non-superpower efforts to build nuclear arsenals. In North Korea, attempts by the United States and others to persuade the government to stop its nuclear program have met with mixed results; in Iraq, Saddam Hussein's nuclear ambitions have been quashed only temporarily.

The hearing's dismal tone was set by the first speaker, Adele Simmons, president of the John D. MacArthur Foundation and an expert in international affairs. Simmons predicted that "more violence at levels we cannot imagine is in store."

The risk of an atomic weapon detonating somewhere on Earth has grown.

But the specific Doomsday times that the witnesses suggested, along with their explanations, were as different as fission and fusion:

• Midnight. Bradford Lyttle, editor of the *Midwest Pacifist Commentator,* said that "the players should stop playing the game" and that "nuclear arsenals be deactivated at once."

• 11:58. Theodore Taylor, a repentant former fission bomb designer-turned-activist, focused on "grossly insufficient" security leading to the possibility that terrorists could construct weapons of mass destruction.

If it were just national governments that had access to plutonium, Taylor said, the clock could be moved back to 11:30. But "no system of safeguards," he added, "could provide absolute assurance against violations of bans." He advocated the elimination of nuclear materials, facilities and weapons.

• 11:51. Arjun Makhijani, a nuclear fusion expert with the Maryland-based Institute of Energy and the Environment, blamed the spread of dangerous plutonium on U.S. government funding pushed by members of Congress for their home districts. "The Trojan horse carrying a nuclear device should be depicted as a pork barrel," Makhijani joked.

• 11:40. Gloria Duffy, who headed the Pentagon's disarmament assistance to the former Soviet Union, was heartened by the retraining of Russian weapons scientists, the dismantling of the nation's weapons and a surrender by Ukraine to Russia of weapons that had belonged to the Soviet Union.

• 10:00. University of Chicago political scientist John Mearsheimer alone defended the bomb, calling it the "ideal middle-class weapon." He called atomic bombs "a source of peace, not war," because of their deterrent effect. A minor-country conflict, he said, is more likely than a major-nation exchange. (He suggested a separate clock—set at around 11:45, to illustrate the risk of a nuclear clash between, say, India and Pakistan.)

"Most Americans," he assured his audience, "like nuclear weapons."

Atomic bombs [are] "a source of peace, not war."

In the end, the board agreed unanimously with the pessimists. "We are still in a nuclear world," said board Chairman Leonard Reiser, a former Manhattan Project scientist.

With 35,000 warheads still threatening, with no treaties in progress, the board hoped to send a message to a complacent U.S. government and a weary public: The nuclear threat continues.

Reiser stretched an arm out to the shiny white minute hand and moved it three spaces ahead.

2

The United States Must Meet Its Nuclear Arms Control Obligations

Lee Butler

Lee Butler, now a retired general, was commander in chief of the U.S. Strategic Command at Offnut Air Base in Nebraska. He was responsible for all U.S. Air Force and Navy strategic nuclear forces until his retirement in 1994.

It was once believed that the power of nuclear weapons prevented the Cold War animosities between the United States and the Soviet Union from escalating into a real war. Now that the Cold War has ended, however, it is easier to see the terrible risks and unjustified costs of maintaining a nuclear arsenal. Belief in nuclear deterrence—the concept that nations with nuclear weapons will not deploy them against one another out of fear of nuclear retaliation—jeopardized the one thing it proclaimed to accomplish: the survival of the United States. If either the Soviet Union or the United States had deployed a nuclear bomb against the other, the attacked nation would have retaliated, resulting in the destruction of both countries. Participation in the nuclear arms war obscured moral reasoning and distorted humanity; the United States and the Soviet Union placed all of the earth's people at risk of annihilation based on the specious argument that nuclear weapons were needed for their respective national defense systems. The use of nuclear weapons can be clearly seen today as indefensible.

I intend to address two matters that go to the heart of the debate over the role of nuclear weapons: why these artifacts of the cold war continue to hold us in thrall; and the severe penalties and risks entailed by policies of deterrence as practised in the nuclear age.

It is distressingly evident that for many people nuclear weapons retain an aura of utility, of primacy and of legitimacy that justifies their existence well into the future. The persistence of this view, which is per-

Reprinted with permission from "Death by Deterrence," by Lee Butler, *Resurgence*, March/April 1999.

fectly reflected in the announced modification of US nuclear weapons policy in 1999 [the United States has resumed testing missiles for a national defense system and has initiated the Stockpile Stewardship Program to maintain its nuclear arsenal], lies at the core of the concern that moves me so deeply. This abiding faith in nuclear weapons was inspired and is sustained by a catechism instilled over many decades by a priesthood which speaks with great assurance and authority. I was for many years among the most avid of these keepers of the faith in nuclear weapons. Like my contemporaries, I was moved by fears and fired by beliefs that date back to the earliest days of the atomic era. We lived through a terror-ridden epoch punctuated by crises whose resolution held hostage the saga of humankind. For us, nuclear weapons were the saviour that brought an implacable foe to his knees in 1945 and held another at bay for nearly half a century. We believed that superior technology brought strategic advantage, that greater numbers meant stronger security, and that the ends of containment justified whatever means were necessary to achieve them.

[The cold war] was in every respect a modern-day holy war, a cosmic struggle between the forces of light and darkness.

These are powerful beliefs. They cannot be lightly dismissed. Strong arguments can be made on their behalf. Throughout my professional military career, I shared them, I professed them and I put them into operational practice. And now it is my burden to declare with all of the conviction I can muster that in my judgement they served us extremely ill. They account for the most severe risks and most extravagant costs of the US-Soviet confrontation. They intensified and prolonged an already acute ideological animosity. They spawned successive generations of new and more destructive nuclear devices and delivery systems. They gave rise to mammoth bureaucracies with gargantuan appetites and global agendas. They incited primal emotions, spurred zealotry and demagoguery, and set in motion forces of ungovernable scope and power. Most importantly, these enduring beliefs, and the fears that underlie them, perpetuate cold-war policies and practices that make no strategic sense. They continue to entail enormous costs and expose all humankind to unconscionable dangers. I find that intolerable. Thus I cannot stay silent. I know too much of these matters: the frailties, the flaws, the failures of policy and practice.

The nuclear arena

The moment I entered the nuclear arena I knew I had been thrust into a world beset with tidal forces, towering egos, maddening contradictions, alien constructs and insane risks. Its arcane vocabulary and apocalyptic calculus defied comprehension. Its stage was global and its antagonists locked in a deadly spiral of deepening rivalry. It was in every respect a modern-day holy war, a cosmic struggle between the forces of light and darkness. The stakes were national survival, and the weapons of choice were eminently suited to this scale of malevolence.

As my own career progressed, I was immersed in the work of all these cultures, either directly in those of the Western world, or through penetrating study of communist organizations, teachings and practices. My responsibilities ranged from the highly subjective, such as assessing the values and motivation of Soviet leadership, to the critically objective, such as preparing weapons for operational launch. I was engaged in the labyrinthian conjecture of the strategist, the exacting routines of the target planner and the demanding skills of the aircrew and the missilier. I have been a party to their history, shared their triumphs and tragedies, witnessed heroic sacrifice and catastrophic failure of both men and machines. And in the end I came away from it all with profound misgivings.

Ultimately, as I examined the course of this journey, as the lessons of decades of intimate involvement took greater hold on my intellect, I came to a set of deeply unsettling judgements. That from the earliest days of the nuclear era, the risks and consequences of nuclear war have never been properly weighed by those who brandished it. That the stakes of nuclear war engage not just the survival of the antagonists, but the fate of humankind. That the likely consequences of nuclear war have no politically, militarily or morally acceptable justification. And, therefore, that the threat to use nuclear weapons is indefensible.

These judgements gave rise to an array of inescapable questions. If this be so, what explained the willingness, no, the zeal, of legions of cold warriors, civilian and military, not just to tolerate but to multiply and to perpetuate such risks? By what authority do succeeding generations of leaders in the nuclear weapons states usurp the power to dictate the odds of continued life on our planet? Most urgently, why does such breathtaking audacity persist at a moment when we should stand trembling in the face of our folly and united in our commitment to abolish its most deadly manifestation?

I have no other way to understand the willingness to condone nuclear weapons except to believe they are the natural accomplice of visceral enmity.

These are not questions to be left to historians. The answers matter to us now. They go to the heart of present-day policies and motivations. They convey lessons with immediate implications for both contemporary and aspiring nuclear states. As I distil them from the experience of three decades in the nuclear arena, these lessons resolve into two fundamental conclusions.

First, I have no other way to understand the willingness to condone nuclear weapons except to believe they are the natural accomplice of visceral enmity. They thrive in the emotional climate born of utter alienation and isolation. The unbounded wantonness of their effects is a perfect companion to the urge to destroy completely. They play on our deepest fears and pander to our darkest instincts. They corrode our sense of humanity, numb our capacity for moral outrage, and make thinkable the unimaginable. What is anguishingly clear is that these fears and enmities are no respecters of political systems or values. They prey on democracies and totalitarian societies alike, shrinking the norms of civilized behaviour and dimming the prospects for escaping the savagery so powerfully imprinted in our genetic code. That should give us great pause as we imagine the task of abolition in a world that gives daily witness to acts of unspeakable barbarism. So should it compound our resolve.

The evil empire

The evidence to support this conclusion is palpable, but, as I said at the outset of these remarks, for much of my life I saw it differently. That was a product of both my citizenry and my profession. From the early years of my childhood and through much of my military service I saw the Soviet Union and its allies as a demonic threat, an evil empire bent on global domination. I was commissioned as an officer in the United States Air Force as the cold war was heating to a fever pitch. This was a desperate time that evoked on both sides extreme responses in policy, in technology and in force postures: bloody purges and political inquisitions; covert intelligence schemes that squandered lives and subverted governments; atmospheric testing with little understanding or regard for the long-term effects; threats of massive nuclear retaliation to an ill-defined scope of potential provocations; the forced march of inventive genius that ushered in the missile age arm-in-arm with the capacity for spontaneous, global destruction; reconnaissance aircraft that probed or violated sovereign airspace, producing disastrous encounters; the menacing and perilous practice of airborne alert bombers loaded with nuclear weapons.

By the early 1960s, a superpower nuclear arms race was underway that would lead to a ceaseless amassing of destructive capacity, spilling over into the arsenals of other nations. Central Europe became a powder keg trembling under the shadow of Armageddon, hostage to a bizarre strategy that required the prospect of nuclear devastation as the price of alliance. The entire world became a stage for the US-Soviet rivalry. International organizations were paralysed by its grip. East-West confrontation dominated the nation-state system. Every quarrel and conflict was fraught with potential for global war.

This was the world that largely defined our lives as American citizens. For those of us who served in the national security arena, the threat was omnipresent, it seemed total, it dictated our professional preparation and career progression, and cost the lives of tens of thousands of men and women, in and out of uniform. Like millions of others, I was caught up in the holy war, inured to its costs and consequences, trusting in the wisdom of succeeding generations of military and civilian leaders. The first requirement of unconditional belief in the efficacy of nuclear weapons was early and perfectly met for us: our homeland was the target of a consuming evil, poised to strike without warning and without mercy.

For all of my years as a nuclear strategist, operational commander and public spokesman, I explained, justified and sustained America's massive nuclear arsenal as a function, a necessity and a consequence of deterrence. Bound up in this singular term, this familiar touchstone of security dating back to antiquity, was the intellectually comforting and deceptively simple justification for taking the most extreme risks and the expenditure of trillions of dollars. It was our shield and by extension our sword. The nuclear priesthood extolled its virtues and bowed to its demands. Allies yielded grudgingly to its dictates even while decrying its risks and costs. We brandished it at our enemies and presumed they embraced its suicidal corollary of mutually assured destruction. We ignored, discounted or dismissed its flaws and cling still to the belief that deterrence is valid in a world whose security architecture has been wholly transformed.

An age of deliverance

But now I see it differently. Not in some blinding revelation, but at the end of a journey, in an age of deliverance from the consuming tensions of the cold war. Now, with the evidence more clear, the risks more sharply defined and the costs more fully understood, I see deterrence in a very different light. Appropriated from the lexicon of conventional warfare, this simple prescription for adequate military preparedness became in the nuclear age a formula for unmitigated catastrophe. It was premised on a litany of unwarranted assumptions, unprovable assertions and logical contradictions. It suspended rational thinking about the ultimate aim of national security: to ensure the survival of the nation.

How is it that we subscribed to a strategy that required near perfect understanding of an enemy from whom we were deeply alienated and largely isolated? How could we pretend to understand the motivations and intentions of the Soviet leadership without any substantive personal association? Why did we imagine that a nation which had survived successive invasions and mind-numbing losses would accede to a strategy premised on fear of nuclear war? Deterrence in the cold-war setting was fatally flawed at the most fundamental level of human psychology in its projection of Western reason through the crazed lens of a paranoid foe. Little wonder that intentions and motives were consistently misread. Little wonder that deterrence was the first victim of a deepening crisis, leaving the antagonists to grope fearfully in a fog of mutual misperception. While we clung to the notion that nuclear war could be reliably deterred, Soviet leaders derived from their historical experience the conviction that such a war might be thrust upon them and if so, must not be lost. Driven by that fear, they took Herculean measures to fight and survive no matter the odds or the costs. Deterrence was a dialogue of the blind with the deaf. In the final analysis it was largely a bargain we in the West made with ourselves.

> *[Belief in nuclear deterrence] suspended rational thinking about the ultimate aim of national security: to ensure the survival of the nation.*

Deterrence was flawed equally in that the consequences of its failure were intolerable. While the price of undeterred aggression in the age of uniquely conventional weaponry could be severe, history teaches that nations can survive and even prosper in the aftermath of unconditional defeat. Not so in the nuclear era. Nuclear weapons give no quarter. Their effects transcend time and place, poisoning the Earth and deforming its inhabitants for generation upon generation. They leave us wholly without defence, expunge all hope for meaningful survival. They hold in their sway not just the fate of nations, but the very meaning of civilization.

Deterrence failed completely as a guide in setting rational limits on the size and composition of military forces. To the contrary, its appetite was voracious, its capacity to justify new weapons and larger stocks unrestrained. Deterrence carried the seed, born of an irresolvable internal contradiction, that spurred an insatiable arms race.

Mutually assured destruction

I was part of all that. I was present at the creation of many of these systems, directly responsible for prescribing and justifying the requirements and technology that made them possible. I saw the arms race from the inside, watched as intercontinental ballistic missiles ushered in mutually assured destruction and multiple warhead missiles introduced genuine fear of a nuclear first strike. I participated in the elaboration of basing schemes that bordered on the comical and force levels that in retrospect defied reason. I was responsible for war plans with over 12,000 targets, many struck with repeated nuclear blows, some to the point of complete absurdity. I was a veteran participant in an arena where the most destructive power ever unleashed became the prize in a no-holds-barred competition among organizations whose principal interest was to enhance rather than constrain its application. And through every corridor, in every impassioned plea, in every fevered debate rang the rallying cry, deterrence, deterrence, deterrence.

Deterrence is a slippery conceptual slope. It is not stable, nor is it static; its wiles cannot be contained. It is both master and slave. It seduces the scientist yet bends to his creation. It serves the ends of evil as well as those of noble intent. It holds guilty the innocent as well as the culpable. It gives easy semantic cover to nuclear weapons, masking the horrors of employment with siren veils of infallibility. At best it is a gamble no mortal should pretend to make. At worst it invokes death on a scale rivalling the power of the creator.

Is it any wonder that at the end of my journey I am moved so strongly to retrace its path, to examine more closely the evidence I would not or could not see? I hear now the voices long ignored, the warnings muffled by the still-lingering animosities of the cold war. I see with painful clarity that from the very beginnings of the nuclear era, the objective scrutiny and searching debate essential to adequate comprehension and responsible oversight of its vast enterprises were foreshortened or foregone. The cold light of dispassionate scrutiny was shuttered in the name of security, doubts dismissed in the name of an acute and unrelenting threat, objections overruled by the incantations of the nuclear priesthood.

The penalties proved to be severe. Vitally important decisions were routinely taken without adequate understanding, assertions too often prevailed over analysis, requirements took on organizational biases, technological opportunity and corporate profit drove force levels and capability, and political opportunism intruded on calculations of military necessity. Authority and accountability were severed, policy dissociated from planning, and theory invalidated by practice. The narrow concerns of a multitude of powerful interests intruded on the rightful role of key policy-makers, constraining their latitude for decision. Many were simply denied access to critical information essential to the proper exercise of their office.

At best [nuclear deterrence] is a gamble no mortal should pretend to make. At worst it invokes death on a scale rivalling the power of the creator.

Over time, planning was increasingly distanced and ultimately disconnected from any sense of scientific or military reality. In the end, the nuclear powers, great and small, created astronomically expensive infrastructures, monolithic bureaucracies and complex processes that defied control or comprehension. Only now are the dimensions, costs and risks of these nuclear nether worlds coming to light. What must now be better understood are the root causes, the mindsets and the belief systems that brought them into existence. They must be challenged, they must be refuted, but most importantly, they must be let go.

Misplaced faith

Sad to say, the cold war lives on in the minds of those who cannot let go the fears, the beliefs, and the enmities born of the nuclear age. They cling to deterrence, clutch its tattered promise to their breast, shake it wistfully at bygone adversaries and balefully at new or imagined ones. They are gripped still by its awful willingness not simply to tempt the apocalypse but to prepare its way.

What better illustration of misplaced faith in nuclear deterrence than the persistent belief that retaliation with nuclear weapons is a legitimate and appropriate response to post-cold-war threats posed by weapons of mass destruction? What could possibly justify our resort to the very means we properly abhor and condemn? Who can imagine our joining in shattering the precedent of non-use that has held for over fifty years? How could America's irreplaceable role as leader of the campaign against nuclear proliferation ever be re-justified? What target would warrant such retaliation? Would we hold an entire society accountable for the decision of a single demented leader? How would the physical effects of the nuclear explosion be contained, not to mention the political and moral consequences? In a singular act we would martyr our enemy, alienate our friends, give comfort to the non-declared nuclear states and impetus to states who seek such weapons covertly. In short, such a response on the part of the United States is inconceivable. And as a nation we have no greater responsibility than to bring the nuclear era to a close. Our present policies, plans and postures governing nuclear weapons make us prisoner still to an age of intolerable danger. We cannot at once keep sacred the miracle of existence and hold sacrosanct the capacity to destroy it. We cannot hold hostage to sovereign gridlock the keys to final deliverance from the nuclear nightmare. We cannot withhold the resources essential to break its grip, to reduce its dangers. We cannot sit in silent acquiescence to the faded homilies of the nuclear priesthood. It is time to reassert the primacy of individual conscience, the voice of reason and the rightful interests of humanity.

3

Nuclear Disarmament Would Threaten the Security of the United States

Stephen Chapman

Stephen Chapman is a columnist and editorial writer for the Chicago Tribune. *His twice-weekly column on national and international affairs appears in some sixty papers across the country.*

Retired general Lee Butler and sixty other retired generals have recently called for the complete elimination of nuclear weapons. This proposal is impossible and dangerous. The knowledge required to build nuclear weapons exists and will always exist. Even if the countries that now possess nuclear weapons were to disarm, other countries will use existing knowledge to develop nuclear capabilities. National and international security is best achieved under the specter of nuclear arms because the threat of annihilation forces all countries to act cautiously. The United States is safer with a nuclear arsenal than without it.

In 1928, world leaders signed the historic Kellogg-Briand Pact, which outlawed war forever. Alas, it didn't put an end to military conflict. But its failure didn't put an end to utopian fantasies, either.

One of those dreams is a nuclear-free world, which has been around as long as nuclear weapons. Recently, it has been championed by a seemingly unlikely group—60 retired generals and admirals from around the world who signed a manifesto calling for the "complete and irrevocable elimination of nuclear weapons."

Nuclear weapons make the world safe

Their chief spokesman is retired Gen. Lee Butler, former head of the Strategic Air Command, the military's nuclear arm, who has been lionized for an address in January 1997 in Washington urging worldwide nuclear disarmament. That speech, says the *New York Times*, "has had an im-

Reprinted from "A World Without Nuclear Weapons?" by Stephen Chapman, *Conservative Chronicle*, February 5, 1997. Reprinted with permission of Stephen Chapman and Creators Syndicate.

pact comparable to the diplomat George F. Kennan's classic article on containing Communism, published in *Foreign Affairs* magazine in July 1947." By Butler's account, the response from both the public and his former colleagues in the military has been overwhelmingly positive.

If so, it has also been overwhelmingly wrong. Ridding the world of nuclear weapons, like ridding the world of war, is an impossible task. And even if it were possible, it would be a fool's errand. Nuclear weapons are here to stay, and the world is a safer place as a result.

The technology has been around for half a century, has been exploited by at least 10 different nations and is firmly lodged in the minds of thousands of scientists scattered all over the world. So accessible is the essential information that back in the 1970s, an obscure American political magazine was able to produce an accurate article on how to build an H-bomb. Trying to purge such knowledge from the human mind is like trying to disinvent fire. It can't be done.

True, all the existing nuclear powers could scrap their doomsday stockpiles. But that wouldn't prevent a rogue state like Libya, Iraq or North Korea, or some terrorist fanatics, from assembling a bomb. And in an otherwise nuclear-free world, anyone with a couple of these weapons, and the apparent willingness to use them, would hold vast coercive power over any government it chose to target. With our current nuclear arsenal, an Iraqi bomb would be a problem. With no nuclear arsenal, it would be a catastrophe.

They work because they are horrific

Everything Gen. Butler and his fellow critics say about nuclear weapons is true. They are horrifically destructive; they have no practical military use; they are impossible to defend against; and they hold us all hostage to the possibility of sudden apocalypse. But the disarmament advocates are wrong to see those qualities as terrible flaws. In fact, they are the very virtues that make nuclear weapons indispensable. Nuclear weapons are so unimaginably fearsome that no one wants to take the risk of precipitating their use—which makes for peace and stability. A nuclear world is a cautious world.

Butler says the United States could only gain from nuclear abolition because "our conventional superiority is unapproachable." But tanks and F-16s are not a substitute for H-bombs. Nuclear weapons are a far more effective deterrent to war than all the conventional arms on Earth could ever be. A nation's leader can imagine winning a conventional war: Though the cost may be high, his country could gain enough in power, resources and security to justify the sacrifice.

Nuclear weapons are here to stay, and the world is a safer place as a result.

The idea of victory in a nuclear war, by contrast, is perfectly insane. A nuclear exchange means annihilation for both sides—swift, certain and total. Faced with that sobering reality, aggressors are inhibited not just from launching nuclear attacks on other nuclear nations but also from launching conventional attacks. The risks are too great.

The United States and the Soviet Union were the two largest and best-equipped adversaries in human history. They didn't remain at peace for all those years because they liked each other but because they feared each other. Knowing they could destroy each other, they were careful to avoid a shooting war of any kind, anywhere. A nuclear-free world would be much more prone to conventional war among great powers—which, as two world wars proved, can be monstrously devastating in its own right.

The idea of victory in a nuclear war . . . is perfectly insane. A nuclear exchange means annihilation for both sides.

Abolishing nuclear weapons wouldn't abolish the age-old sources of human conflict; it would merely given them freer rein. Butler says the existence of nuclear weapons "condemns the world to live under a dark cloud of perpetual anxiety." It may come as news to the disarmers that human beings have always lived under the perpetual threat of war. Nuclear weapons have done far more to relieve that anxiety than to provoke it.

4

The United States Should Ratify the Comprehensive Nuclear Test Ban Treaty

Madeleine Albright

Madeleine Albright is the U.S. secretary of state.

The Cold War has ended but danger to the United States posed by nuclear weapons has not. To decrease this danger, the United States should ratify the Comprehensive Nuclear Test Ban Treaty (CTBT), which would prohibit all signatories from testing nuclear weapons. The CTBT would increase international security by impeding the development of nuclear weapons by nuclear weapons states and constraining the nuclear capabilities of non-nuclear states. Critics of the CTBT argue that some signatories will ignore the treaty and continue to develop and test nuclear weapons. There will be far less cheating than critics fear, however, because cheaters can be easily detected, and once discovered, will be penalized under international law. Furthermore, signing the treaty will not undermine the security of the United States, as treaty opponents claim, because even without testing, the United States can maintain its nuclear arsenal. The Senate's failure to ratify the CTBT in 1999 has led other countries to suspect that the United States is abandoning international security efforts—a lack of confidence that could lead to increased nuclear proliferation and pose security risks to the United States.

Editor's Note: Madeleine Albright's remarks were given before the Chicago Council on Foreign Relations, Chicago, Illinois, on November 12, 1999.

I would like to discuss with you a major part of [the United States' responsibility to prevent the next century from being bloodier than the last]. Because even though the Cold War has ended, the dangers posed to us by nuclear weapons have not. We must carry out a comprehensive

Excerpted from "Americans Must Unite to Reduce the Dangers Posed by Nuclear Weapons," speech delivered by Madeleine Albright before the Chicago Council on Foreign Relations, Chicago, November 12, 1999.

strategy to limit those dangers both by keeping such weapons out of the wrong hands and by deterring and defending against their possible use.

These goals received a setback in October 1999, when the U.S. Senate voted not to ratify the Comprehensive Nuclear Test Ban Treaty, or CTBT.

America's allies and friends responded to this vote with universal shock and disappointment. I have personally been besieged by calls from my counterparts around the globe. All express concern. Some even fear that America is on the verge of deciding simply to go it alone, to abandon efforts at nuclear nonproliferation, and to rely solely on military might in what could become a new, wider, and even more dangerous nuclear arms race. My reply to those who harbor such fears is not to overreact. The United States has not gone crazy.

If we do not accept the rules we insist that others follow, others will not accept them either.

If you remember 1991, Iraq's president Saddam Hussein invaded another country. He pillaged it; he set fire; and he decided that he could control the region. Before that, he had gassed his own people. He had been acquiring weapons of mass destruction.

We carried out, with the help of an alliance, a war in which we put Saddam Hussein back in his box. The United Nations voted a set of resolutions which demanded that Saddam Hussein live up to his obligations and get rid of the weapons of mass destruction. The United Nations Security Council imposed a set of sanctions on Saddam Hussein until he did that. It also established an organization.

So there was an organization that was set up to monitor whether Saddam Hussein had gotten rid of his weapons of mass destruction. That organization, UNSCOM [United Nations Special Commission], has made clear he has not. The United States, in the person of me, in fact, authored a resolution—because I was concerned about the children of Iraq—to make sure that Saddam Hussein would be able to sell his oil for food and medicine.

There has never been an embargo against food and medicine. It is just that Saddam Hussein has not chosen to spend his money on that. Instead, he has chosen to spend his money on building weapons of mass destruction and palaces for his cronies; in fact, I think he has built 54 palaces at more than $2 billion since the war ended.

We have established a regime which would make sure that the food and medicine is distributed to the children of Iraq. And where the UN is active in northern Iraq, child mortality has gone down. It is Saddam Hussein who is keeping his people in bondage. It is Saddam Hussein who gassed his own people. It is not the United States or the United Nations.

Okay. My reply to those who harbor the fear that we might overreact and pull out of the world is that the United States has not gone crazy. A clear majority in the Senate wanted to delay voting to allow more time to deliberate on the treaty. President Bill Clinton and Vice President Al Gore have reaffirmed America's commitment to nonproliferation. And, as Winston Churchill once reportedly declared, "Americans can always be counted upon to do the right thing in the end, after all the other possibilities have been exhausted."

Sharply divided

That said, the Senate debate was a highly sobering experience. Never before have the clearly expressed views of our closest allies been so lightly dismissed; never before has the Senate rejected so abruptly a treaty of this importance; and never before has the tradition of a bipartisan foreign policy—once championed by such giants of this state as Everett Dirksen and Paul Douglas—seemed so distant.

Much has been said about how the Administration and Senate leadership handled this issue. It is fair to assign blame to both sides: to the Senate for giving the treaty short shrift; to the Administration for not doing enough to lay the groundwork for a successful debate.

But our focus now must be not on where we have been but on where we are headed. That is why I have chosen to address this subject. . . . Those of us in public life have a duty—when circumstances warrant—to raise a flag of warning. And I do so now, because I believe it is dangerous when the world's leading nation is as sharply divided as we appear to be on how to confront the world's greatest threat.

Our challenge is to overcome the scars left by past arguments, put aside partisan distractions, and come together around concrete measures that will keep Americans secure. To succeed, we must go beyond slogans to the reality of a world in which U.S. actions and attitudes have real consequence. Because if we do not accept the rules we insist that others follow, others will not accept them either. The result will be a steady weakening of nuclear controls. If efforts at control fail, within a couple of decades or less, a host of nations from the Middle East through South Asia to the Korean Peninsula could possess nuclear weapons and the ability to deliver them at long range.

One can imagine then a world imperiled by bitter regional rivalries in which governments are able to threaten and destroy each other without ever having to mass troops at a border, send an aircraft aloft, or launch a ship of war.

A test ban would create security

This is where the issues of nuclear testing and missile defense are linked, for those of us concerned about defending against missiles armed with weapons of mass destruction should be the first to value halting nuclear tests as an initial line of defense.

More than four decades ago, President Dwight Eisenhower warned that the knowledge of how to build nuclear weapons would spread and that not even a massive arsenal would be enough to keep America safe. He strived, therefore, to achieve agreements, including a comprehensive test ban, that would reduce the risk of war.

His successor, President John Kennedy, took up that same banner. In 1963, he said that

the conclusion of a treaty to outlaw nuclear tests . . . would check the nuclear arms race in one of its most dangerous areas. . . . Surely, this goal is sufficiently important to require our steady pursuit, yielding to the temptation neither to give up the effort, nor . . . our insistence on vital and responsible safeguards.

These, then, are the core principles that guided America in years past and should guide us still.

First, America must lead in the effort to assure stability and peace in a nuclear world.

Second, we should strive for sound agreements to reduce the dangers posed by nuclear weapons.

Third, we should view such agreements not as ends, but as means; they must contribute to our overall security.

If [nuclear tests] were to happen, the world, not just the United States, would object with the full force of international law on its side.

Obviously, agreements do not erase the need for a powerful nuclear and conventional military deterrent, but they establish rules that increase the chance that our deterrent will succeed in preventing war; they complicate efforts by potential adversaries to develop and build nuclear weapons; and they make it more likely that others will join us in a common response against those who break the rules.

By outlawing nuclear tests, the CTBT will impede the development of more advanced weapons by nuclear weapons states and constrain the nuclear capabilities of countries that do not now have such weapons. For example, in Asia, the CTBT would make it harder for North Korea to advance its nuclear weapons program or for China to develop the technology required to place multiple warheads atop a single small missile.

In the Persian Gulf, the treaty would create another important yardstick to measure the intentions of Iran, where a historic debate between the forces of openness and isolation is underway. In South Asia, the treaty would be a valuable tool for constraining a potentially catastrophic arms race along a disputed border.

In Russia, there is support among some for building a new generation of tactical nuclear arms, because Russia's conventional military capabilities have degraded, and money is lacking to rebuild them. The CTBT would reinforce momentum towards nuclear restraint around the world.

Cheaters would be detected

Despite these benefits, critics say the treaty is too risky because some countries might cheat. But improvements in our own national means of verification, together with the International Monitoring System established by the treaty, would enhance our ability to detect nuclear explosions. Also, the treaty's provisions for on-site inspections should help deter violations and assist in finding the smoking gun should a violation occur.

Moreover, the military value of very low-yield tests is limited. They are of little use in developing more advanced strategic weapons.

The bottom line is that, under the CTBT, it is less likely that nations will test because the risks of detection will be higher. But if they do test in ways that might threaten our security, they will be detected. And if that were to happen, the world, not just the United States, would object with the full force of international law on its side.

Of course, some among you may ask, so what? Aren't international law and world opinion merely abstractions? Won't governments, and especially those we worry about most, pursue their own interests regardless of treaty obligations?

There is a good deal of merit in these questions. But there is no merit to the conclusion that some draw—which is that if we cannot assure 100% compliance with the rules we establish, we are better off not establishing any rules at all. Consider the facts.

During the first 25 years of the nuclear age, five countries tested nuclear weapons. In the 29 years since, two—India and Pakistan—have joined the list. During this period, knowledge about how to build nuclear arms has spread, but far fewer nations than we once predicted are acting on that knowledge.

Most nations disapprove of nuclear arms

The question is "Why?" The answer, I think, is that global standards matter. Over the years, more and more nations have embraced the view that it is unnecessary and dangerous to develop and test nuclear weapons. This view has given birth to an extensive, although not yet complete, framework of legally binding agreements. These include nearly universal participation in the nuclear Non-Proliferation Treaty, or NPT.

Of course, neither law nor opinion will prevent nations from acting in their own best interests. But most countries are influenced in how they define their interests by what the law is, and most find it in their interests to operate within the law or, at least, be perceived as doing so.

Why else, for example, did South Africa, Brazil, and Argentina abandon their nuclear weapons programs? Why else did China agree to halt its own nuclear tests and sign the CTBT? Why else have India and Pakistan agreed, in principle, to do the same? And why else have the nations that contribute to the proliferation problem made such vigorous efforts at concealment?

Some treaty opponents have pointed out, accurately, that North Korea joined the NPT and then evaded its obligations under it. But why did North Korea take on these obligations in the first place? And why should we conclude that because that pact was violated, we would have been safer without it? After all, North Korea's secret activities first came to light as a result of inspections under that agreement.

Further, we can only imagine what kind of world we would have today if the NPT had not entered into force three decades ago. Or what kind of world we will have three decades from now if we decide that the job of stopping proliferation is either not worth doing or already done.

To me, it is an open and shut case that outlawing nuclear tests by others will result in a more favorable security climate for America than would otherwise exist. But the second question we must consider is whether accepting a legal ban on our own tests will undermine our nuclear deterrent.

Deterrent not harmed

That deterrent includes our ability to put a nuclear weapon on a bomber or missile and deliver that weapon with a high degree of accuracy. The knowledge that we can do this will stop any rational government from attacking us, and the CTBT would not affect that. Because the treaty does not cover delivery systems, we can continue to test and modernize them.

There can be no doubt that our deterrent is effective. After all, we have already conducted more than 1,000 tests—hundreds more than anyone else. Our knowledge base and technology are superb. However, many Senators opposed the CTBT because of their concern that, without testing, weapons in our arsenal might become either unsafe or unreliable.

Obviously, this is a very serious concern, which we have taken seriously. Our nation's most experienced nuclear weapons scientists have examined very carefully the possibility that our weapons will degrade without testing. They have recommended steps that will enable us to retain confidence in the safety and reliability of our arsenal under CTBT, including a robust program of stockpile stewardship. These steps were incorporated in a package of understandings that accompanied the treaty when it was submitted to the Senate.

We simply do not need to test nuclear weapons to protect our security. On the other hand, would-be proliferators and modernizers must test if they are to develop the kind of advanced nuclear designs that are most threatening. Thus, the CTBT would go far to lock in a technological status quo that is highly favorable to us.

The United States can withdraw

There is, moreover, even another layer of protection for American security. If the day should come when our experts are not able to certify the safety or reliability of our nuclear arsenal—or if the treaty is not working and new threats are arising that require us to resume nuclear tests—we will have the right to withdraw from the treaty.

The case for ratifying the CTBT is strong. It asks nothing of us that we cannot safely do; it requires of others a standard we very much want the world to meet. Those tempted to cheat will face a higher risk of being caught and will pay a higher price when they are. And if the worst case unfolds and we must withdraw, we can and will.

The burden on treaty supporters is to persuade skeptics that ratifying the CTBT will reduce the dangers posed to our security by nuclear weapons, without endangering our security by preventing us from taking steps necessary to national defense.

But there is also a burden on treaty opponents, for it is not sufficient simply to say the treaty is imperfect, opponents must offer an alternative that is better. And they must explain why America will be safer in a world where nuclear tests are not outlawed and may again become commonplace, where there is no guarantee of an international monitoring system to detect such tests, where we have no right to request on-site inspections, and where America is held responsible by allies and friends everywhere for the absence of these protections.

To those Senators who want the Administration to bury the CTBT, we say, no, our national interests will not allow us to do that. But to those who are willing to take a further look at the treaty, we say, how can we help? For despite the Senate vote, the treaty lives.

It is essential that the dialogue on CTBT continue and bear fruit. After all, the Administration and Congress have worked together on difficult national security issues before. A number of leading Senators from both parties have expressed interest in a bipartisan effort to move forward on CTBT now.

Bridging differences

In that spirit, I am announcing today that we will establish a high-level Administration task force to work closely with the Senate on addressing the issues raised during the test ban debate. As we did with NATO enlargement, this team will also carry the dialogue to Americans from all walks of life to explain and analyze the treaty.

In our discussions with the Senate, we will be open to a variety of possible approaches for bridging differences, including at an appropriate point the potential need for additional conditions and understandings, as was the case with the Chemical Weapons Convention.

Meanwhile, President Clinton has made clear that the United States will continue to observe a moratorium on nuclear explosive tests and has urged all others to do the same. And we will continue to work with Congress to provide our share of support for preparatory work, including construction of the International Monitoring System.

Finding the way forward on CTBT is necessary, but not sufficient, to crafting a bipartisan strategy for reducing the nuclear danger. It is equally important that we establish common ground on the question of national missile defense and the Anti-Ballistic Missile Treaty [known as the ABM, the treaty was signed by the United States and the former Soviet Union in 1972; it outlawed the construction of nuclear defense systems].

Here, agreement must be found between the extremes. On one side, there are those demanding that we scrap the ABM Treaty, despite objections from Russia, China, and our closest allies. On the other are people who oppose any adjustments to the treaty and are against developing even a limited system of national missile defense.

The Administration believes that both extreme views are dangerous. The first risks reviving old threats to our security; the second fails to respond to new ones.

The ABM contributes to nuclear security

For more than a quarter-century, the ABM Treaty has contributed to strategic nuclear stability. It is based on the understanding that an all-out competition in ABM systems would create destabilizing uncertainties about intentions and destroy our ability to reduce strategic offensive arms. Preserving this understanding is vital to us. It is also essential to Russia.

If we were simply to abandon the ABM Treaty, we would generate fears in Moscow that we are also abandoning the goal of stability; we would squander an historic opportunity for negotiating further mutual reductions in our nuclear arsenals; and we would run the unnecessary risk of transforming Russia into once again our most powerfully armed adversary.

On the other hand, our partners must recognize that the strategic environment has changed greatly in the 27 years since the ABM Treaty was signed. The Gulf War showed what a real threat theater-range missiles in hostile hands can be. And tests of longer range missiles by Iran and North Korea raise concerns about vulnerability that must be addressed.

Our military serves as an effective deterrent to any rational adversary. The problem is how to deal with threats from sources that are neither rational nor interested in complying with global norms.

It is against this danger that the Administration is developing and testing a limited National Missile Defense System, with a decision on deployment possible as early as next summer. For deployment to occur, certain changes to the ABM Treaty would be necessary, and we have begun discussing these with Congress, our allies and Moscow.

Global standards matter.

To date, Russian leaders have expressed strong opposition to any treaty modifications and accused us of undermining the entire system of international arms control simply by raising the subject. A Russian defense official recently proclaimed that his nation has the ability to overwhelm the missile defense system we are planning. That is true—and part of our point. The system we are planning is not designed to defend against Russia and could not do so. And that will remain true even if we are able to negotiate further deep reductions in our arsenals.

The changes we are contemplating in the ABM Treaty are limited. They would not permit us to undermine Russia's deterrent. And because Russia and the U.S. are vulnerable to the same threats, we are prepared to cooperate with Moscow on missile defense.

In response, Russia must do more than just say *nyet*. It is in our mutual interest to develop an arrangement that preserves the essential aims of the ABM Treaty, while responding to the new dangers we both face.

Domestically, the Administration recognizes that if we are to have support for any agreement we might reach with Russia, we must consult closely with the Legislative Branch. The Administration and Congress have the same boss—and that is . . . the American people. We have an obligation to work shoulder to shoulder in support of policies that will keep our citizens secure.

In defending against nuclear dangers, we rely on a combination of force and diplomacy. That is why our military must remain second to none, but also why we need resources to back our international diplomatic leadership. Earlier in 1999, Congress voted to cut the President's request for international programs by more than $2 billion. By standing firm in our negotiations, we won much of that back.

Now we are engaged in a final effort to persuade Congress to pay what we owe to the United Nations. This is not just a matter of honoring our word, although that in itself should be enough.

The UN serves important American interests. These include peace-keeping, safeguarding nuclear materials, prosecuting war criminals, enforcing sanctions against rogue states, protecting intellectual property rights, fighting disease, and saving children's lives.

A half-century ago, our predecessors created the United Nations. Thirty-eight years ago, our nation was proudly represented there by Illinois' favorite son—Adlai Stevenson. Today, we are the organization's number one debtor. We are even in danger of losing our vote in the UN General Assembly. America can do better than that. I hope you agree. Congress should vote this year—at long last—to pay our UN bills.

The issues I have discussed . . . of nuclear risks and national defense, of resources and American interests affect us all. And I hope the dialogue concerning them will broaden far beyond the narrow corridors of Washington, DC.

These are matters that warrant the attention of our universities and scientists, our professionals, and our vast network of nongovernmental organizations. We need a truly national debate.

We Americans are the inheritors of a tradition of leadership that has brought our country to the threshold of the new century strong and respected, prosperous, and at peace. The question our children will ask is whether we were good stewards of that inheritance.

A decade or two from now, we will be known as the bitter partisans who allowed their differences to immobilize America or as the generation that marked the path to a safer world. We will be known as the unthinking unilateralists who allowed America's international standing to erode or as the generation that renewed our nation's capacity to lead.

There is no certain roadmap to success, either for individuals or for nations. Ultimately, it is a matter of judgment, a question of choice.

[The CTBT] asks nothing of us that we cannot safely do; it requires of others a standard we very much want the world to meet.

In making that choice, let us remember that there is not a page of American history of which we are proud that was authored by a peddler of complacency or a prophet of despair. We are a nation of doers.

We have a responsibility in our time, as others have had in theirs, not to be prisoners of history but to shape history; a responsibility to act—with others when we can, alone when we must—to protect our citizens, defend our interests, preserve our values, and bequeath to future generations a legacy as proud as the one we received from those who came before. To that mission, I pledge my own best efforts and summon both your support and the wise counsel of this esteemed Council.

Thank you very much for your attention.

5

A Ban on Nuclear Testing Would Weaken the U.S. Defense System

Andrew Lewis

Andrew Lewis hosts a nationally syndicated radio show, "The Andrew Lewis Show," which provides analysis on current events.

The purpose of the U.S. defense policy is to protect American lives. Ratifying the Comprehensive Test Ban Treaty (CTBT)—which prohibits the testing of nuclear weapons—would undermine U.S. defenses because it bans the procedures necessary to maintain the aging nuclear arsenal of the United States. Nuclear arms are vital to protect the United States from dangerous countries like Russia and China that would sign the treaty but would later circumvent it. As a global moral leader, the United States has a right to protect itself; only with a strong international presence will the United States be strong enough to defend its allies from the nuclear threats of countries that are hostile to democratic ideals. In refusing to ratify the treaty, the United States strengthened its role as an international sentry protecting freedom and world peace.

On October 13, 1999, fifty-one Senate Republicans voted to reject the Comprehensive Test Ban Treaty (CTBT). The treaty, signed by President Bill Clinton in 1996, would prohibit nuclear weapons testing of any kind. Its rejection has ignited a firestorm of criticism; the Republicans have been condemned for everything from damaging America's status as a "global moral leader" to encouraging a rebirth of the nuclear arms race.

In reality, however, their vote reflects a last vestige of Americanism in the Senate.

The CTBT's supporters claim that America's ratification would be a major step towards total nuclear disarmament and world peace. All of the world's forty-four nuclear-capable nations must sign and ratify the treaty before it takes effect. American ratification, it was claimed, would renew pressure on other "dilatory" countries to follow suit. What are these other

Reprinted with permission from "The Test Ban Treaty: Poison, Not Antidote," by Andrew Lewis, *The Intellectual Activist*, December 1999.

nations? India, Pakistan, and North Korea have not signed the CTBT at all, and Russia and China are among the 15 signatory nations who have not ratified the treaty.

The fact that North Korea, Russia, and China are among the countries who are supposedly awaiting America's lead is reason enough *not* to ratify the treaty; these countries should be required to be the *first* to disarm. But whether or not America's ratification would encourage global nuclear disarmament is irrelevant. The purpose of a proper American defense policy is not to engage in futile attempts to eradicate a technology that has already spread to the rest of the world. Its purpose is to protect American lives.

Many reasons not to ratify

Senate Republicans, led by John Kyl and Jesse Helms, argued persuasively against the treaty, primarily on two grounds. First, they argued that the CTBT could not be enforced effectively, citing recent reports by the Central Intelligence Agency that challenged the reliability of monitoring systems. More important, they pointed out that testing is necessary to maintain America's nuclear arsenal. As our nuclear weapons age, we have to discover how this affects their strength and reliability—and computer-modeling, which has been suggested as the alternative to testing, is no substitute for direct experimentation.

However true, even these arguments do not identify the central issue. A treaty such as the CTBT—which America undoubtedly would follow assiduously while other nations circumvent it—sacrifices our capacity to develop and maintain the weapons necessary to defend ourselves and to deter whatever threats may exist or emerge.

To be truly the world's moral leader—and even to increase the chances of world peace—the United States must assert its *moral* right to its own defense. Under no circumstances—particularly in cooperation with hostile nations—should America hobble its capacity for self-defense by limiting itself to current technology and computer models.

Increasingly, America's international treaties and commitments have weakened both our international "moral status" and our defenses. Our moral status is not that of a leader, but that of a craven coward unwilling to do anything that might upset international opinion.

The purpose of a proper American defense policy . . . is to protect American lives.

In the *reductio ad absurdum* of this policy, President Clinton tried to compensate for the failure of the CTBT by proposing that, in order to enhance our defenses, we should fund and assist with *Russia's* defense system. The 1972 Antiballistic Missile (ABM) Treaty, negotiated with the Soviet Union, prohibits the establishment of a national anti-missile defense system. Ostensibly, this treaty was signed to prevent either America or the Soviet Union from accumulating or developing missiles sufficient to breach such a system. (A likelier explanation is that the Soviet Union agreed to both in order to shackle America's superior technology and to divert much needed funds to its own disastrous economy.) In other words, committing to a weaker defense system was argued to be "safer" than building a stronger one.

Consequently, the missile-defense systems now being successfully tested by our military can only be deployed in a limited manner, protecting only part of the country. In exchange for renegotiating the ABM Treaty to allow a wider deployment, Clinton proposed that the United States help Russia to complete one of *its* missile-tracking radar systems, and upgrade another, at the cost of many millions of dollars.

China and Russia unite

Russia, it must be remembered, still possesses thousands of strategic missiles. The Russian parliament has never ratified the START II treaty on arms limitation and is already working with China—the second most dangerous country in terms of missile quantity—to bring the collective weight of the United Nations against American attempts to renegotiate the ABM treaty. In other words, the crumbling remnant of history's most totalitarian state and the only remaining communist nation of any strategic significance, are lobbying against the freest nation's right to defend itself.

A treaty such as the Comprehensive Test Ban Treaty—which America undoubtedly would follow assiduously while other nations circumvent it— sacrifices our capacity to . . . defend ourselves.

Given this context, America's status as a "global moral leader" is, if anything, enhanced by the CTBT's rejection. It is evidence that America is not yet completely willing to subordinate its national sovereignty to global opinion, and that we have the right to determine independently what is proper for our defense.

However, because the crucial principle of America's right to defend itself remains unstated, our self-imposed moratorium on testing continues and the next Senate may ratify the CTBT. Not only should the CTBT be torn up, but so too should the START II agreement, the ABM treaty, and every other arms control agreement that infringes on America's right to self-defense. Morality requires that the first—and last—country of freedom stand sentry over the rights of its citizens and sacrifice nothing that would protect them.

6

The United States Should Deploy an Effective Nuclear Missile Defense System

James H. Anderson

James H. Anderson is a research fellow at the Heritage Foundation, a public policy think-tank. He is the author of America at Risk: The Citizen's Guide to Missile Defense.

The United States should deploy a national nuclear missile defense system in order to protect itself and its allies from proliferating nuclear threats. Danger from nuclear disaster has increased because missile capabilities have advanced worldwide and deterrence-oriented strategies that depended upon a rational opponent such as the former Soviet Union will be ineffective against new, irrational enemies such as Iraq. A nuclear defense system will cost less today than it did during the Cold War, can be updated as better technologies are developed, and would not violate the Anti-Ballistic Missile Treaty since that treaty became defunct with the disintegration of the Soviet Union.

In 1998, the American Legion passed a resolution supporting the deployment of a national missile defense system—a timely measure given the proliferation of ballistic missiles in the Third World. Yet despite this growing threat, and the danger of an accidental or unauthorized launch from Russia and China, the United States presently has no ability to intercept missiles aimed at its cities.

Third World missile capabilities have increased dramatically in recent years. In August 1998, North Korea tested the Taepo Dong-l, a three-stage rocket with the potential to reach parts of Hawaii and Alaska. North Korea is building the next generation ballistic missile, the Taepo Dong-2, an even longer-range missile capable of reaching America's West Coast.

North Korea is not the only rogue state America has to worry about. According to intelligence estimates, more than 20 states are developing ballistic missiles. Ballistic missiles have become *de rigueur* for states seek-

Reprinted with permission from "National Missile Defense: An Insurance Policy for the Future," by James H. Anderson, *American Legion Magazine*, December 1999.

ing to offset America's prowess on the battlefield. America's crushing defeat of Iraqi forces in Kuwait during Operation Desert Storm in 1991 convinced many would-be aggressors it would be unwise to challenge the United States conventionally; NATO's [the North Atlantic Treaty Organization] punishing air campaign against Yugoslavia in 1999 will probably reinforce this conclusion.

Third World leaders also are attracted to ballistic missile programs because of their relatively low cost. Ballistic missiles are cheaper than maintaining other delivery systems, such as manned bombers. In addition, dictators find missiles attractive because they can exercise tight operational control over them.

Post–Cold War deterrence

Deterring the threat of missile attack is more problematic now than it was during the Cold War. Back then, the United States deterred Soviet aggression with the threat of reprisal. Today America is faced with a more diverse array of threats, ranging from accidental or unauthorized launch by Russia or China to emerging Third World capabilities.

Deterrence based on retaliation presumes one's opponent will act rationally. History, however, indicates the opposite is true. During World War II, for example, Nazi Germany and Imperial Japan fought on long after it was clear they would lose.

Today America is faced with a more diverse array of threats, ranging from accidental or unauthorized launch by Russia or China to emerging Third World capabilities.

Looking to the future, it would be unwise to assume the threat of retaliation will always suffice to dissuade Third World states from attacking. Missile defense should be considered a prudent form of insurance against deterrence failing. "It is . . . folly not to take every step we possibly can to defend ourselves against a possible attack from Russia, China, North Korea, Iran and Iraq," says Caspar Weinberger, former Secretary of Defense. "As we have seen . . . India and Pakistan are deploying ballistic missiles and North Korea has unleashed this three-stage missile over Japan."

The United States will pay a terrible price if deterrence fails and an enemy missile destroys an American city. The damage in human and material terms would dwarf that of any natural disaster the United States has suffered. Even absent an actual attack, America's vulnerability to missile attack will undermine its ability to honor security commitments abroad. President George Bush's response to Iraq's invasion of Kuwait in 1990 probably would have been different if Saddam Hussein had possessed missiles capable of striking the United States.

Critics of national missile defense charge it would be too costly. In the 1980s, one estimate, often repeated by the media, pegged the cost of former president Ronald Reagan's Strategic Defense Initiative program at $1 trillion. Today, the projected costs of deploying a multi-layered defense are much less. Taking into account current budget projections, most proposals for building a national missile defense system would consume roughly two or three percent of defense expenditures annually.

The decline in costs is two-fold. First, early critics of Reagan's research program exaggerated some of the initial cost estimates. Second, computer chips are becoming faster, more sophisticated and cheaper every year. These advances generally favor defensive technologies designed to locate, track and intercept ballistic missiles.

Use available technology

Opponents of missile defense also claim deploying a system now would waste money because better technology will be available in the future. By this rationale, however, the time for actual development will never be ripe. A police chief who decided to withhold bulletproof vests from his patrol officers because more technologically advanced vests were being researched would not last five minutes in office.

Congress should insist on a deployment plan that makes the best use of technologies available now and those expected to be available in the near future. Intercept tests conducted this year with the advanced Patriot and Theater High Altitude Area Defense anti-missile systems have already demonstrated the United States' hit-to-kill capability. America should move swiftly to test national systems capable of protecting the country against missile attack. As with any major military programs, appropriate upgrades to a deployed system should be considered as technology advances.

A properly designed missile defense should be able to anticipate and neutralize potential countermeasures. For example, a defensive system that can intercept enemy missiles shortly after liftoff would destroy them before they could release individual warheads, bomblets and decoys. A national missile defense system also would have inherent self-defense capabilities against the potential of direct attack. For example, sea-based defenses could maneuver to avoid attack. For their part, space-based sensors could be protected against countermeasures by making them maneuverable or perhaps coating them with "stealth" technology to evade detection.

The ABM Treaty is defunct

Critics also charge deployment of a national missile defense would violate the 1972 Anti-Ballistic Missile [ABM] Treaty, which prohibited the construction of nationwide defenses. This charge would be true if the treaty were still in force. But this Cold War agreement was linked inextricably with the Soviet Union's unique geographic and legal personality. Yet today neither Russia nor any combination of Soviet successor states is capable of fulfilling the original purposes of the ABM Treaty. This is why numerous scholars and strategists, including ABM architect Henry Kissinger, believe this agreement is legally defunct.

Unfortunately, the administration's attempt to preserve the core of this outdated treaty will likely perpetuate restrictions on the type of national missile defense America needs to deploy. In particular, treaty restrictions will hamper the development of sea- and space-based defenses.

Moving beyond the ABM Treaty will not ruin relations with Moscow, as critics often charge. Moderate Russian leaders have no reason to feel threatened by a defensive system designed to save lives. While Russia's future political course remains uncertain, the United States has a duty to protect its citizens against missile threats, whatever their source. "Ballistic missile defenses, both strategic and theater, can significantly enhance deterrence and crisis stability, increase military capabilities, protect allies, friends and coalitions . . . and improve the conditions for peace in troubled regions," says Ronald Lehman, former director, Arms Control and Disarmament Agency.

With such troubled regions pressing ahead with long-range missile programs, it is neither smart nor fair that America's plans for a national missile defense remain beholden to an outdated treaty.

Use sea- and space-based sites

One current proposal is to build one, possibly two, ground-based sites. This, however, would be far more costly and less effective than sea- and space-based alternatives. A ground-based system would have an extremely narrow window to intercept missiles with multiple warheads and decoys that have separated from their rocket boosters. Even with a successful intercept, deadly fallout from a nuclear, chemical or biological weapon would occur over the United States.

To counter the emerging threat, America should develop defenses to identify, track and shoot down hostile missiles shortly after liftoff, when they are most vulnerable to interceptors and before they can release their deadly cargo. Sea- and space-based defenses hold the greatest promise for achieving this "boost-phase" intercept capability.

The United States will pay a terrible price if deterrence fails and an enemy missile destroys an American city.

To this end, the United States should move rapidly to upgrade the anti-missile capability of the Navy's Aegis defense system, first deployed over a decade ago to protect its fleet. This proposal would not require the construction of any additional ships, for the Navy already has 22 Aegis cruisers.

With appropriate upgrades and modifications, a sea-based system could provide the United States with an initial layer of protection against missile threats. This system also could help protect America's allies. For example, Aegis cruisers in the Mediterranean could shield Western Europe against Iranian missile attacks. Eventually, America could reinforce its sea-based defenses with space-based interceptors to provide its citizens with an additional layer of protection.

News, not fiction

The threat of ballistic missile attack from Third World states is not a Hollywood fantasy or a plot in a Tom Clancy novel. The loss of a single city to a nuclear-tipped missile would dwarf the damage caused by the terrorist strikes on the World Trade Center and the federal building in Oklahoma City.

As long as the United States remains defenseless, future dictators will seek the capacity to threaten the lives of millions of Americans with long-range missiles. "I believe there is a threat today," says Gen. John Piotrowski, former commander in chief of the Space Command. "I believe that as long as we have no defense against ballistic missiles, it makes them very attractive to people who either want to blackmail us or wish us ill."

The United States will be forced to think twice about honoring security agreements abroad because of its own vulnerability at home. Fortunately, technological advances have made national missile defense both affordable and practical. Prudence dictates that the United States deploy an effective national missile defense before rogue states acquire missiles capable of destroying American cities.

7

Deployment of a National Missile Defense System Threatens Nuclear Security

John Steinbruner

John Steinbruner is director of the Center for International and Security Studies and a professor in the School of Public Affairs at the University of Maryland.

The push to deploy a National Missile Defense (NMD) system—an arsenal of missiles capable of targeting and destroying any nuclear missiles descending on the United States—is motivated by politics, not technical or strategic requirements, and ignores the threat that such a system would have on the security of the United States. Deploying a NMD system would enable other countries to design nuclear weapons that could evade U.S. defenses. Furthermore, in establishing a NMD system, the United States would break the Anti-Ballistic Missile Treaty—a move that would provoke hostile international reaction. Russia in particular is likely to perceive an NMD system as a threatening measure and would likely react by developing more sophisticated nuclear weapons.

On July 22, 1999 President Bill Clinton signed legislation proclaiming it to be the policy of the United States to deploy a national missile defense (NMD) system "as soon as technologically possible." The stated purpose is to protect all U.S. territory against limited ballistic missile attacks launched deliberately by "rogue" opponents. An additional purpose widely inferred is to defend against an accidental or unauthorized missile launch from any source. In his accompanying statement, the president noted that the expression of intent did not yet authorize an actual deployment or appropriate funds to carry it out. He indicated, however, that he would make a specific deployment decision by July 2000 and promised to take technical performance and threat assessments, as well as all the costs and arms control implications of a deployment program, into account.

Reprinted with permission from "National Missile Defense: Collision in Progress," by John Steinbruner, *Arms Control Today*, November 1999.

Politics over national security

At the time of that announcement, the design of an NMD system had not been completed and no intercept tests had been conducted. The first such test occurred on October 2, 1999 and demonstrated that the final-stage homing mechanism could intercept a target warhead traveling at intercontinental-range speed (7 kilometers/second) when placed on a near-collision course under ideal conditions. But that test was directed against an unrealistically cooperative target, and the homing mechanism, known as the exoatmospheric kill vehicle (EKV), was the only major component of the eventual system involved. The first integrated test involving the radar and information management components of the envisaged system will occur in the spring of 2000, and even that test will use a surrogate booster rocket. Only three of the 19 intercept tests expected to be necessary for full system development are currently anticipated before July 2000, and the full sequence is not expected to be completed until 2005. Nonetheless, NMD development program officials are suggesting that the as-yet-unspecified and untested system might achieve its initial operating capability in 2005.

There is no realistic prospect that a [national missile defense] system could perform as advertised over the foreseeable future.

This schedule is widely assumed to have been inspired by domestic politics, since it makes no sense in technical or strategic terms. As indicated by the carefully limited character of the October test, the intercept technology is not ready for operational application, and it will clearly require more than the year allotted to make a reasonable technical judgment about overall system performance. Meanwhile, none of the alleged rogues have actually initiated deployment of ballistic missiles capable of reaching the United States. The principal suspect, North Korea, has held only two tests of a missile incapable of delivering even a very small payload over intercontinental distances and has announced an indefinite moratorium on further tests pending the outcome of negotiations with the United States to terminate their program. To deploy an inadequately tested defensive system before an offensive threat is realized virtually guarantees that any threat which does subsequently appear will be able to penetrate the system. It is a disadvantage in this game to make the first technical commitment and irresponsible to do so without some form of restraint on the opposing offense—the equivalent of using antibiotics indiscriminately and thereby generating drug-resistant strains.

Why indulge in such behavior? The generally inferred answer is that President Clinton is determined to avoid a direct confrontation with congressional Republicans on the topic lest their assertive advocacy of an NMD program provide a significant partisan advantage in the upcoming presidential election. By extension of that supposition, it is assumed that the decision made in July 2000 will be arranged to sound like a deployment commitment, whatever hedges might be built into it. Prevailing

judgment on Washington political circuits holds NMD to be inevitable—
an assertion generally accepted by the national press.

International reactions

There are some inescapable implications of the announced commitment,
however, that are serious enough to put the eventual outcome very much
in doubt. There is no realistic prospect that an NMD system could perform as advertised over the foreseeable future—a couple of decades or
more. Even at the outer edges of plausible success, missile intercept systems cannot expect to keep pace over that period of time with projected
improvements in offensive capabilities. Anyone seriously in the business
of deploying ballistic missiles can be expected to adopt penetration techniques sufficient to get through a rudimentary NMD system. Those sufficiently concerned could also arrange to bypass the system using readily
available cruise missile technology or various methods of clandestine
weapons delivery. Those who are very intensely concerned could develop
the capacity to negate the system by attacking its sensors. So evident are
those facts that potential opponents of the United States are virtually certain to impute a far more ominous intention to an NMD deployment effort. It will be seen as cover for an effort to enhance the already imposing
offensive capacities of the United States, and reactions will predictably be
driven by that interpretation.

That perspective will weigh particularly heavily on Russia and China,
whose assessments of the situation are potentially the most consequential. Both maintain nuclear deterrent forces based primarily on ballistic
missiles that are implicitly directed against the United States. Both do so
at substantial disadvantage. Russia inherited a large force from the Soviet
Union with thousands of weapons nominally available but without the
current financial assets or the longer-term economic base necessary to
sustain that force. China has relied all along on a much smaller force of
some 20 missile launchers not maintained on immediate alert status.
When it comes down to daily operating conditions, both of these forces
are in principle quite vulnerable to an attack initiated by the larger and
technically more capable American nuclear forces.

They have substantial conventional force disadvantages as well. The
sensing systems and information-handling capacity associated with the
projected NMD system would meaningfully enhance the pre-emptive potential of U.S. offensive forces, both nuclear and conventional. Even the
limited initial deployment of 100 interceptors designed for 4-to-1 en-
gagements would threaten the residual deterrent forces that Russia and
China could expect to survive an initial U.S. attack. Once the sensors and
information management assets were in place, the number of available
interceptors could be rapidly increased, particularly since the United
States is simultaneously pursuing theater missile defense deployments
that could be adapted to the national defense mission. Rapid expansion
of the initial system would bring the United States to the threshold of a
decisive disarming capability under which, in theory, the credibility of
China's small deterrent force and Russia's deteriorating one would collapse completely. Summary dismissal of these concerns by official U.S. in-
terlocutors and the failure of domestic political discussion to credit them

is seen by Russia and China as indication of American disingenuousness—an impression that significantly compounds the problem.

North Korea's assessments are also consequential but on a different scale because North Korea is not remotely capable of waging a sustained military confrontation with the United States, as Russia and China might conceivably manage to do if given no other option. With a small, isolated, deteriorating economy and a society in obvious internal peril, North Korea has to fashion some form of accommodation as a matter of the most basic survival. And despite the rogue image routinely imposed upon it—an image that it has historically done a great deal to deserve—the North Korean government has indicated serious interest in accommodation since the 1994 signing of the Agreed Framework, an accord that effectively terminated its production of fissionable material. As a natural extension of that initiative, North Korea has expressed a willingness in principle to eliminate its ballistic missile program in exchange for appropriate compensation, and the test moratorium announced in September 1999, is certainly consistent with such an intention, if not yet a guarantee. As a practical matter, by the time a U.S. NMD deployment might actually be completed, North Korea is unlikely to exist in its current form. If it does survive, it will mostly likely have done so by achieving a broad accommodation with the United States that decisively restrained its missile development efforts. In the very unlikely event that the North Korean regime manages to hang on while maintaining "rogue" status, then they will presumably have mastered penetration techniques along with the other basic features of missile technology. Like Russia and China, such a North Korea would have strong reason to worry about the offensive implications of a U.S. NMD effort, but there would be less they could do about it.

It would be exceedingly difficult for either military planners or political leaders in Russia and China to accept [the] danger [of a national missile defense system].

At this point it is impossible to determine with any confidence how these three countries—or any of the others inherently threatened by a U.S. NMD effort—would actually react to an NMD deployment. They themselves have probably not yet made that determination. It is very apparent, however, that the situation presents those states with a severe policy dilemma that is bound to have serious consequences. If they choose to accept the U.S. NMD effort under the rationale that it is only a limited system, they can avoid immediate political confrontation and play for time, hoping that the United States will eventually acknowledge their legitimate concerns after realizing NMD's technical difficulties and strategic implications. However, that approach locks in a rationale and accepts a momentum of U.S. investment that will inexorably lead to increasing military inferiority. In a future conflict, such a stark disadvantage could be decisive. It would be exceedingly difficult for either military planners or political leaders in Russia and China to accept that danger. If, on the other hand, the major rivals and alleged rogues assertively defend their longer-term security interests, they could find themselves in an immediate political confrontation with the United States that would seriously disrupt their efforts to work out productive terms of economic engagement. A conflict between security and economic interests is as agonizing a problem as the world of policy has to offer, and when driven into desperate circumstances, people do desperate things.

U.S. allies will probably not fully credit the fears of potential opponents, but they are likely to comprehend their dilemma and will assuredly want to dampen its consequences. However popular romantic images of national missile defense might be in the United States, they will not sweep the world, and in the end, world opinion does matter for the United States.

Impending collision

At the moment, the United States and Russia are on a collision course over this issue. The U.S. NMD program unambiguously contradicts the 1972 ABM [Anti-Ballistic Missile] Treaty, and Russia would have to agree to enabling amendments in order to legalize the effort. Otherwise, the United States would have to formally withdraw from the treaty or simply violate it in order to proceed with an actual deployment. The United States has proposed amendments that would accommodate the first phase of the projected program by validating the system's national coverage and providing for an interceptor site and enhanced radar facility in Alaska. It is also apparent that at subsequent phases of the program, the United States would have to ask for treaty amendments allowing both for improvements and new construction at five existing ground-radar installations and new construction at four additional sites. And it is expected that the eventual system will depend on a new network of infrared sensors deployed in space, a provision that would also require a treaty amendment and is certain to be of particular concern to Russia. Once completed, these facilities would clearly provide the basis for rapid deployment of a larger number of interceptors and a more capable overall system.

Although [past] Russian President Boris Yeltsin has agreed in principle to discuss ABM Treaty adjustments, it is evident that Russian military analysts do not consider even the initially suggested amendments to be acceptable because they do not believe Russia can tolerate the projected deployment. Reported offers by the United States to assist in the completion of two radar installations will not make a meaningful difference in their judgment, which the Russian political system is unlikely to override. Implied U.S. threats to withdraw from the treaty if the amendments are not accepted are generally considered in Russia to be an ultimatum they cannot responsibly accept. Consensus opinion in Russia holds that the abandonment of the ABM Treaty would invalidate all of the offensive force limitation agreements. As a practical matter that amounts to a counter-ultimatum.

There is no plausible resolution of the impasse yet in sight, and a direct legal collision appears imminent. Russia could make a legal case that the October test in connection with the July legislation is already a violation of the ABM Treaty. If a deployment commitment is made in July

2000, even provisionally, construction for the interceptor site in Alaska is scheduled to begin in the spring of 2001, and the United States itself admits that pouring concrete at that site would violate the current terms of the treaty. With that in mind, close observers of the situation are freely speaking of a train wreck in progress. Given the U.S. Senate's vote against ratification of the Comprehensive Test Ban Treaty, it is not difficult to visualize catastrophic consequences—the cascading failure not only of the ABM Treaty but of START I, START II [treaties between the United States and Russia that mandate a reduction in both countries' nuclear arsenal; START I has been ratified by both countries, but START II has yet to be ratified by Russia], and ultimately the Nuclear Non-Proliferation Treaty [which prohibited any nation that did not have nuclear arms from obtaining them] itself. That sequence would be a major crisis of international security and could shake the U.S. alliance system to its foundations.

In the wake of the Cold War, there is a monumental imbalance in military capability throughout the world, with U.S. allies enjoying much greater protection.

Although life is notoriously uncertain and occasionally generates miraculous escapes at the last moment, it is prudent to assume that the impending collision will not be avoided within the framework of current policy. The specific issues in question are embedded in a much broader set of security problems that cannot be resolved by the sort of marginal deals currently being discussed by the official negotiators. In the wake of the Cold War, there is a monumental imbalance in military capability throughout the world, with U.S. allies enjoying much greater protection against traditional threats than any others. This inherent discrimination is very difficult to justify or to sustain even among the current alliance members for a very practical reason: it imposes unmanageable burdens on the major societies not included—dangerously unmanageable ones in the case of Russia.

Russia needs reassurance

Russia's economic base is currently assessed at less than 2 percent of the United States', and it is plagued with deep structural problems highly related to the Soviet Union's ultimately unsuccessful effort to keep pace with Western military development. There is no socially feasible economic reform program yet devised that would plausibly deal with this problem, and as a result, there is no realistic prospect for rapid and sustained expansion of Russia's economic base. An unavoidable implication is that the Russian government does not have adequate financial assets to perform any of its major functions, including support of its 1.2 million-person military establishment. That establishment has been financially starved under the Russian Federation and has been progressively deteriorating for a decade. It is nonetheless responsible for what is inherently one of the most demanding security missions in the world: defense of a

20,000-kilometer perimeter, with NATO to the west and China to the east. None of the military's central missions can be performed to the standards of traditional contingency planning. No international security arrangement provides direct assistance of meaningful consequence.

Faced with an overall security problem that is essentially unmanageable in traditional terms, Russia has drifted, inevitably one might say, into comprehensive reliance on the deterrent effect of nuclear weapons to cover virtually all major security missions. But even that is not an assured redoubt. The nuclear weapons component of the Russian military establishment will deteriorate and, at any rate, is destined for financial reasons to be substantially smaller and less capable than that of its major potential opponent—the United States. In this context, the implicit threat that the U.S. NMD program poses to the highly beleaguered Russian deterrent force has very broad and very powerful resonance.

It would be unlikely under any circumstance that declarations of benign intent, however sincere and however formally expressed, would provide what Russian military planners could reasonably consider to be adequate reassurance. But even that precarious possibility has been severely prejudiced by recent history. The Soviet government that allowed German unification to occur in a swift and graceful manner believed it had been assured that NATO would not subsequently extend its jurisdiction eastward. Nonetheless, NATO quickly proceeded to do so and currently talks as if it will continue the project. In the course of its expansion process, NATO assured the Russian government that it was exclusively a defensive alliance and would never attack unless one of its members was first attacked. But a scant two years after Russia formally acceded to NATO expansion, thus granting the appearance of a consensual process, NATO conducted an air assault against Yugoslavia despite vehement Russian opposition. It did so, moreover, at its own initiative with no attempt whatsoever to secure approval from the UN Security Council, where Russia would have had legal standing to object. In the aftermath, NATO believes its action to have been fully justified, while Russia sees the entire exercise not only as a breach of promise and a violation of international legal procedure, but also as an implicit threat to Russia itself. As a result of this sequence, NATO as a whole, the United States included, has seriously undermined its ability to credibly reassure Russia for quite some time.

It is not yet evident—mercifully, perhaps—whether or when the accumulating pressures on Russia will produce a catastrophic breakdown or how such a breakdown would be manifested. It is quite evident, however, that through its actions the world as a whole is flirting with that dangerous possibility. The combination of intractable security burdens and perceived provocation makes the impending collision over the ABM Treaty very perilous indeed.

Imaginable outcomes

With major elections scheduled in both the United States and Russia, there is a strong presumption that neither government can manage any major policy initiative before 2001, and there is no public indication that either government is considering one. Both election campaigns can be expected to encourage assertive nationalism and to suppress any inclination for accommodation of the scope required. Nonetheless, hopeful speculation is not completely pointless. Precisely because the danger is considerably more serious than currently admitted, there is an occasion for constructive statesmanship, and it is worth considering how it might be accomplished.

The simplest answer is a judicious delay. Despite the mantra of inevitability currently being chanted by most of the political pundits in Washington, NMD deployment is not a sure thing. It would not require all that great a feat of political leadership to point out to the sensible, but always distracted, American majority that the zealots on this subject are far outside of rational bounds. The NMD program will obviously not be ready for a responsible decision on deployment for several years because adequate testing will not have been done and also because the diplomacy necessary to legitimize it clearly cannot be accomplished by July 2000. To pretend otherwise is to assure failure both of the program and of the diplomacy. Majority opinion is evidently prepared for such a message; when asked, most people are vaguely in favor of missile defense but do not consider it a major priority. They surely do not want to pay an exorbitant price in economic, political, legal and strategic terms for a system that will not work anytime soon.

Russia sees the [national missile defense system] not only as a breach of promise and a violation of international legal procedure, but also as an implicit threat to Russia itself.

But postponement alone is not an enduring answer, and it is questionable whether restoration of the traditional answer—indefinitely restricted defense to preserve nuclear deterrence at lower force levels—can endure either. Regardless of the presence or absence of national missile defense in the United States, Russia cannot safely sustain the large, highly alert deterrent operations inherited from the Cold War. The pre-emptive damage that the United States and NATO are capable of inflicting on Russian forces virtually precludes the comprehensive forms of retaliation envisaged by traditional deterrence doctrine and virtually compels reliance on rapid-reaction practices to assure even the most minimal deterrent standard. Russia cannot maintain its forces on rapid-reaction status without running an unreasonable risk of triggering an accidental, unauthorized or inadvertent engagement. The United States is better able to do this, but there is no good reason for either country to preserve a swift and massive deterrent threat. They do it because they have habitually done it, but that is not an acceptable reason. The coupling together of deterrent forces under fallible managerial control is the single greatest danger to both sides. Any residual inclinations for aggression that either side might harbor can readily be deterred by a force configuration that does not maintain any weapons on alert status and is not prepared for massive retaliation. Such an arrangement would emphasize reliable reassurance rather than overwhelming deterrence. It would be a great deal safer than the current situation and as a result would provide superior overall security to both sides and the rest of the world as well. In principle, the transition to that improved state might be initiated through collaboration on missile and aircraft surveillance, a central feature of any NMD effort.

Reassure Russia by sharing information

Basically the process of transition would involve full integration of Russia and eventually of China into the sensing and information management network necessary to support any national missile defense deployment. At a minimum, that means they would reliably receive the surveillance and tracking data generated by the system at the same time as the United States does and would have all the algorithms required to interpret it. That would not give them command authority over U.S. NMD operations but it would give them full vision and intimate involvement. Although they would be unlikely to do so, in principle they could use the information for their own NMD operations and would supply the United States with any data they independently generated.

At first glance—and for sometime thereafter—intimate collaboration of that sort would be considered unimaginable, especially by the most assertive NMD advocates. But despite the prevalence of what might be called standard belligerent attitudes, the United States in fact has inherently powerful interests in such an arrangement. The surveillance of threatening missile trajectories and of air traffic generally is one of the most glaring deficiencies of the current Russian deterrent operation, and it has distinctly dangerous consequences. If the United States is not attacking Russia, we need them to know that with complete confidence at all times, lest confusion trigger Russia's nuclear force, which is poised for rapid reaction because of its inherent vulnerability. Although we might be supremely confident about our own benign intentions, it would be the height of arrogance—potentially fatal arrogance—to suppose that the Russians are as confident. At the moment, conveying reliable reassurance is a far greater problem for the United States than preserving reliable deterrence.

> *If the United States is not attacking Russia, we need them to know that with complete confidence at all times, lest confusion trigger Russia's nuclear force.*

Truly comprehensive collaboration in maintaining missile launch and air traffic surveillance is one of the more promising methods for addressing the problem of reassurance. In order to be effective in that regard, joint surveillance would have to be extended to the pre-launch conditions of all nuclear weapons delivery systems, so that the collaborating partners would know beyond question that a pre-emptive attack could not be undertaken without their detecting the preparations well in advance of the time any ballistic missile or other delivery method could actually be launched—a realization in effect of the de-alerting idea that has been tentatively discussed. The most direct method would be to separate warheads from all transport vehicles and to store them with attached devices that confirm that status, but the principle could be embodied in many different ways. If residual deterrence and not disarming pre-emption is in fact the only intention the United States has, then comprehensive joint surveillance is a strong mutual interest, as is a deterrent force configuration that removes all weapons from alert status. Joint surveillance extended to pre-launch conditions would be a verification arrangement for such a force configuration.

At the moment the U.S. political system clearly does not understand the problem of reassurance and is not willing to consider the measures necessary to address it. The impending collision over NMD might well be the occasion for some enlightenment, however. In the end, the passion of national missile defense, if it is in fact a passion, cannot be satisfied unless comprehensive reassurance is practiced and the operational configuration of offensive forces in whatever residual numbers is transformed accordingly. That would in fact be a much better security arrangement. If the conditions of decisive reassurance could be achieved, including the transformation of offensive forces, there would still be a practical question as to whether a limited or not-so-limited national defense deployment is worth the expense and effort involved, but under those conditions, that would be a relatively harmless question. Under existing conditions, the question is certainly not harmless. It is in fact exceedingly dangerous.

8

Rogue Nations and Terrorist Groups Threaten Nuclear Security

John Deutch

John Deutch is director of the Central Intelligence Agency of the United States.

Nuclear materials and technology are today more available to terrorist groups and rogue nations—countries such as Iraq that do not
obey international law—due to the dissolution of the Soviet
Union. Thieves and terrorists are obtaining nuclear materials because many nuclear sites located in the former Soviet Union are
now unguarded—or guarded by poorly paid Russian workers who
illegally sell the materials in order to make money. Well-
established illegal trade routes and trade networks maintained by
organized crime syndicates across Europe make it difficult to stop
the diversion of nuclear materials into the hands of power-seeking
governments and terrorist groups.

How serious a threat is the potential acquisition of nuclear materials or
even nuclear weapons by states hostile to the U.S. or by terrorists intent on staging incidents harmful to American interests? The chilling reality is that nuclear materials and technologies are more accessible now than
at any other time in history—due primarily to the dissolution of the Soviet
Union and the region's worsening economic conditions. This situation is
exacerbated by the increasing diffusion of modern technology through the
growth of the world market, making it harder to detect illicit diversions of
materials and technologies relevant to a nuclear weapons program.

Russia and the other states of the former Soviet Union are not the
only potential sources of nuclear weapons or materials. The reported theft
of approximately 130 barrels of enriched uranium waste from a storage facility in South Africa demonstrates that this problem can begin in any
state where there are nuclear materials, reactors, or fuel cycle facilities.

A few countries whose interests are inimical to the U.S. are attempting to acquire nuclear weapons—Iraq and Iran being two of the greatest concerns. Should one of these nations, or a terrorist group, get their hands on one or more nuclear weapons, it could threaten or attack deployed American forces or allies, or possibly the U.S. itself.

Years ago, there were two impediments to would-be proliferators: the technical know-how for building a bomb and the acquisition of the fissile material—the highly enriched uranium or plutonium atoms that split apart in a chain reaction and create the energy of an atomic bomb. Today, just the latter applies. While it is by no means easy to make a nuclear weapon, knowledge of weapons design is sufficiently widespread that trying to maintain a shroud of secrecy no longer offers adequate protection.

The security of fissile material in the former Soviet Union thus has become even more critical at the same time it has become more difficult. Many of the institutional mechanisms that once curtailed the spread of nuclear materials, technology, and knowledge no longer exist or are present only in a weakened capacity, and effective new methods of control have yet to be implemented fully for a large portion of the world's nuclear-related materials, technology, and information.

The chilling reality is that nuclear materials and technologies are more accessible now than at any other time in history—due primarily to the dissolution of the Soviet Union.

During the Cold War, the security of Soviet nuclear weapons and fissile material was based on a highly centralized, regimented military system operating within a strong political authority. Nuclear weapons security ultimately depended on a responsible, competent, well-disciplined military establishment at the command and operations level. The breakup of the Soviet Union, the opening of Russian society, and economic difficulties have subjected the security system to stresses and risks it was not designed to withstand. All these changes have worked together to raise both Russian and U.S. concerns about the security of Russian weapons.

The military is facing a crisis situation in housing, pay, food, manning levels, and social services, all of which have resulted in plummeting morale and lapses in discipline. Although nuclear weapons handlers traditionally were among the best-treated and loyal in the Russian military, they now are suffering hardships similar to those of the rest of the armed forces. Meanwhile, the new openness in Russia has reduced the effective distance between personnel who have access to nuclear know-how or weapons and those who may hope to profit from the theft of a nuclear weapon.

The Russian nuclear weapons production complex, and particularly the nuclear material production facilities, face an uncertain future. With the dramatic reduction in nuclear forces that is to occur over the next 10 years, many of the nuclear weapons production facilities will be dismantled or converted to civilian uses.

The once highly regarded personnel employed by these facilities have fewer perks and in some cases their living standards are below that of common factory workers. Some are seeking employment outside the nuclear field, in the commercial sector, where salaries are higher. Some potentially could lose their jobs if work can not be found for them. Moreover, the Ministry of Atomic Energy has told personnel at its facilities that they no longer can rely solely on government funds to support them, and that they need to market their goods and services to remain a viable organization.

In addition to personnel issues, accountability for nuclear materials is a major concern. Tons of weapons-usable material have been distributed over the last 40 years to non-military organizations, institutes, and centers for various nuclear projects. None of these has what the U.S. regards as sufficient accountability. Hundreds of tons more of weapons-usable material will be recovered from the nuclear warhead elimination program as a result of unilateral and multilateral commitments. The accountability system for this material also is uncertain.

The countries of Central Asia and the Caucasus—Kazakhstan, Armenia, Azer-baijan, Kyrgyzstan, and Uzbekistan—form transit links between Asia and the West as well as the Middle East and the West. The breakup of the Soviet Union has resulted in the break-down of the institutions that kept many smugglers and questionable traders out of this region. The pervasive control once exerted by a combination of the KGB, Soviet military, and border guards no longer exists. Even before the breakup, some of the southern borders, especially with Afghanistan, were penetrable. According to recent travelers to these areas, anything can go across the borders in these countries for a minimal price. Border guards can be bribed with as little as a bottle of vodka to allow passage without papers, and a few hundred dollars is all that is necessary to arrange for a carload of goods and travelers to cross without inspection or questions.

There is little hard evidence to support the plethora of unconfirmed reports that this region has been a source of proliferation concern, but weapons of mass destruction, fissile and other radioactive materials, nuclear and missile technology, and scientific expertise are present in the region, and the potential for diversion exists. There is no evidence that existing narcotics transit routes are being used to smuggle nuclear materials. The fact that they are well-established and successful, however, suggests that they easily could be utilized for nuclear materials diversion.

Acquisition of any or all of the critical components of an effective nuclear weapons program—technology, engineering know-how and weapons-usable material—seriously would shorten the time any nation might need to produce a viable nuclear weapon.

Many countries want nuclear weapons

Iran actively is pursuing an indigenous nuclear weapons capability. A wide variety of data indicate that Tehran has assigned civilian and military organizations to support the production of fissile material for nuclear weapons. Specifically, Iran is attempting to develop the capability to produce both plutonium and highly enriched uranium.

In an attempt to shorten the time line to a weapon, it has launched a parallel effort to purchase fissile material, mainly from sources in the former Soviet Union. Iranian agents have contacted officials at nuclear facilities in Kazakhstan on several occasions, trying to acquire nuclear-related materials. In 1992, Iran unsuccessfully approached the Ulba Metallurgical

Plant to obtain enriched uranium. In 1993, three Iranians believed to have had connections to their nation's intelligence service were arrested in Turkey while seeking to acquire nuclear material from smugglers from the former Soviet Union.

Iran's continued nuclear cooperation with Russia and China—even when carried out under international safeguards—indirectly could enhance its technological capabilities for nuclear weapons efforts. It is estimated that Iran is some years away from producing a nuclear weapon, but with extensive foreign assistance or receipt of a significant amount of nuclear materials, Iran could produce a weapon much quicker than if left to its own capabilities.

Iraq remains a formidable nuclear proliferation problem despite its current lack of fissile materials and production facilities. Saddam Hussein built a major program to develop nuclear weapons. Operation Desert Storm significantly damaged its nuclear program as a whole, and United Nations sanctions continue to disrupt Baghdad's progress. Nevertheless, Iraq has not abandoned its nuclear program and repeatedly is taking steps designed to thwart the inspection process.

Iraq remains a formidable nuclear proliferation problem.

The CIA has no indication that Iraq has attempted to acquire fissile material from the former Soviet Union. We assess, however, that Iraq would seize any opportunity to buy nuclear weapons materials or a complete weapon in much the same way it attempted to rejuvenate its missile program in 1995. In that incident, Jordanian authorities intercepted a shipment of sophisticated Russian-produced missile guidance instruments bound for Iraq.

North Korea's nuclear aspirations are of grave concern as well. We assess that North Korea has produced enough plutonium for at least one, possibly two, nuclear weapons. Under the terms of the Oct. 21, 1994, Agreed Framework with the U.S., North Korea agreed to freeze its plutonium production capability. Currently, P'yongyang has halted operation of the 5MW(e) reactor, ceased construction on two larger reactors, frozen activity at the plutonium recovery plant, and agreed to dismantle these facilities eventually. There is no evidence at this time that North Korea has sought to acquire additional fissile material from sources in the former Soviet Union to circumvent the current freeze on its own production facilities.

Libya operates a small Soviet-supplied nuclear research center near Tripoli. Muammar Qadhafi reportedly is trying to recruit nuclear scientists to assist in developing nuclear weapons, although it is doubtful that Tripoli could produce a nuclear weapon without significant foreign technological assistance.

Syria's nuclear research program is at a rudimentary level and appears to be aimed at peaceful uses at this time. It is subject to international Atomic Energy Agency safeguards. At present, we have no evidence that Syria has attempted to acquire fissile material.

Algeria operates two nuclear reactors: one in the capital of Algiers, supplied by Argentina, and a second at Ain Oussera, supplied by China. Aspects of Algeria's nuclear development program cause concern in the West despite claims by Algeria that its reactors are being used for civilian purposes. Algerian scientists could apply the experience gained in running both reactors to a possible future weapons program.

The threat from terrorists

The list of potential proliferators is not limited to states with nuclear weapons ambitions. There are separatist and terrorist groups, criminal organizations, and individual thieves who could choose to further their cause by using fissile or non-fissile (but radioactive) nuclear materials. Despite the number of press articles claiming instances of nuclear trafficking worldwide, there is no evidence that any fissionable materials have been acquired by a terrorist organization. We also have no indication of state-sponsored attempts to arm terrorist organizations with the capability to use any type of nuclear materials, fissile or non-fissile, in a terrorist act. This does not preclude the possibility that a terrorist or other group could acquire, potentially through illicit trading, enough radioactive material to conduct an operation, especially one designed to traumatize a population.

Fissile material would not necessarily be needed for its purposes. Depending upon the group's objectives, any nuclear or radioactive material could suffice. The consequences of a nuclear explosion are well-known, but non-fissile radioactive materials dispersed by a conventional explosive or even released accidentally could cause damage to property and the environment, creating societal and political disruption.

Non-fissionable radioactive materials such as cesium-137, strontium-90, and cobalt-60 can not be utilized in nuclear weapons, but could be used to contaminate water supplies, business centers, government facilities, or transportation networks. Although it is unlikely they would cause significant numbers of casualties, physical disruption, interruption of economic activity, post-incident clean-up, and psychological trauma to a workforce and to a populace would result.

In November, 1995, a Chechen insurgent leader threatened to turn Moscow into an "eternal desert" with radioactive waste. The Chechens directed a Russian news agency to a small amount of cesium-137—a highly radioactive material that can be used both for medical and industrial purposes—in a shielded container in a Moscow park, which the Chechens claimed to have placed. Government spokesmen told the press that the material was not a threat and would need to have been dispersed by explosives to be dangerous. According to Department of Defense assessments, there was only a very small quantity of cesium-137 in the container. If it had been dispersed with a bomb, an area of the park could have been contaminated with low levels of radiation. This could have caused disruption to the populace, but would have posed a minimal health hazard for anyone outside the immediate blast area.

The Japanese cult Aum Shinrikyo, which attacked Japanese civilians with deadly gas on March 20, 1995, also tried to mine its own uranium in Australia and to buy Russian nuclear warheads.

Traditional terrorist groups with established sponsors probably will remain hesitant to use a nuclear weapon for fear of provoking a worldwide crackdown and alienating their supporters. In contrast, a new breed of multinational terrorists, exemplified by the Islamic extremists involved in the bombing of the World Trade Center, might be more likely to consider such a weapon if it were available. These groups are part of a loose association of politically committed, mixed-nationality Islamic militants, motivated by revenge, religious fervor, and a general hatred for the West.

Organized crime is a powerful and pervasive force in Russia today. We have no evidence, however, that large organized crime groups, with established structures and international connections, are involved in the trafficking of radioactive materials. The potential exists, though, and Russian authorities have announced arrests of criminals, alleged to be members of organized crime groups, associated with seizures of non-weapons-grade nuclear materials.

A terrorist or other group could acquire, potentially through illicit trading, enough radioactive material to . . . traumatize a population.

The CIA estimates that there are some 200 large, sophisticated criminal organizations that conduct extensive illegal operations throughout Russia and around the world. These organizations have established international smuggling networks that transport various types of commodities. Many of these groups have connections to government officials that could provide access to nuclear weapons or weapons-grade materials and enhance their ability to transport them out of the country. Various reports suggest there are vast networks, consisting of organized crime bosses, government officials, military personnel, and intelligence and security service officers, as well as legitimate businesses. These networks would have the resources and the know-how to transport nuclear weapons and materials outside the former Soviet Union.

In 1994, European police made the first seizures of weapons-usable material stolen from Russian facilities and smuggled to outside countries. In Germany, they seized about six grams of plutonium, a gram sample of highly enriched uranium (HEU), and approximately a half-kilogram sample containing both plutonium and uranium. Czech police seized just under three kilograms of HEU, the largest quantity yet encountered.

The Russians are working, with U.S. assistance, to improve accountability and control. In addition, they have consolidated many of their warheads in fewer locations and have moved them out of areas of unrest to reduce further the potential for loss. It is estimated that there were more than 500 nuclear storage sites in the former Soviet Union and Eastern Europe in 1990 and that there are less than 100 today, mostly in Russia, with a few remaining in Ukraine, Belarus, and possibly Kazakhstan.

Counterproliferation steps

To combat the proliferation problem, the American intelligence community's efforts have included support to those policy-makers responsible for implementation of the Treaty on the Non-Proliferation of Nuclear

Weapons, wherein the U.S. and other signatories have expressed their nonproliferation commitments, and those implementing the Comprehensive Test Ban Treaty, wherein the U.S. and other signatories have expressed their commitments to end nuclear testing. Moreover, it maintains a surge capability to deploy specialists quickly outside the U.S. to the scene of a terrorist nuclear or radiological threat and to provide advice and guidance on dealing with the situation. During such an event, the specialists would coordinate fully with appropriate U.S. government agencies, keeping them informed and drawing upon their expertise if follow-up action is required.

Organized crime is a powerful and pervasive force in Russia today.

As the threat of proliferation has increased, U.S. intelligence capabilities to support counterproliferation efforts have been redirected or expanded and include:

• Assessing the intentions and plans of proliferating nations.

• Identifying nuclear weapons programs and clandestine transfer networks set up to obtain controlled materials or launder money.

• Supporting diplomatic, law enforcement, and military efforts to counter proliferation.

• Providing direct support for multilateral initiatives and security regimes.

• Overcoming denial and deception practices set up by proliferators to conceal their programs.

• Formation of the Nonproliferation and Arms Control Technology Working Group to enhance the coordination of research and development (R&D) efforts among intelligence, operational, policy, and other elements of the U.S. government.

• Work on the Technical Intelligence Collection Review to identify future shortfalls in sensors against delivery systems activities. This review addresses the 1994 NonProliferation Review Committee identification of technical and operational needs to increase warning times before foreign targets achieve actual operational weapons of mass destruction (WMD) capability.

• Fostering the development of new technologies with the potential to improve ability to detect WMD activities at significantly longer ranges than possible today. For example, the CIA has explored the efficacy of high-risk, high-payoff counterproliferation-related R&D initiatives.

• Reorganizing intelligence activities to increase and sharpen the focus of counterproliferation-related efforts—both analytically and operationally.

• Redirecting resources and activities toward assisting Federal Bureau of Investigation and U.S. Customs Service efforts to identify, target, and apprehend individuals engaged in the trafficking and smuggling of nuclear materials worldwide.

These initiatives have enhanced the ability of the intelligence community to pursue aggressively efforts to uncover hidden supply lines and stop key materials and technologies from reaching countries of proliferation concern. The U.S., in cooperation with other governments, has been able to halt the transfer of a large amount of equipment that could be used in developing nuclear weapons programs, including mass spectrometers, custom-made cable equipment, graphite materials, aluminum melting furnaces, arc-welding equipment, and a gas jet atomizer.

More can, and must, be done. This is not the time to relax. We need to put forth our greatest effort to keep nuclear materials out of the hands of groups or individuals who would inflict damage on the world. We are at a significant juncture in history. Now is the time for all elements of our government to pull even closer together and act in concert with our allies to combat the proliferation of nuclear materials.

9

China Is a Threat to Nuclear Security

Gary Milhollin

Gary Milhollin is a professor at the University of Wisconsin Law School and director of the Wisconsin Project on Nuclear Arms Control, a long-term program to develop a common vision for international leaders on how to reduce the risks posed by nuclear weapons.

China's export of missiles and nuclear technology to Pakistan, Saudi Arabia, and Iran is currently the gravest threat to nuclear security. Pakistan, for example, may decide to use nuclear weapons against its enemy, India, who will surely retaliate with nuclear force. Iran is likely to use the nuclear weapons it develops against its long-term enemy, the United States, and may possibly share its technology with other countries inimical to the United States. Ironically, the nuclear technology exported by China is often obtained directly from the United States through legal purchases. For example, the U.S. company Silicon Graphics recently sold China a super-computer capable of designing sophisticated nuclear weapons technology. Clearly the United States must tighten controls over its exports to China and refuse to certify China as a trading partner until China gives up its nuclear trade to other countries.

I will direct my remarks to three subjects: First, China's exports to countries that are trying to make weapons of mass destruction; second, the strategic impact of American exports to China; and third, nuclear cooperation between the United States and China.

China's exports to proliferant countries

Today, China's exports are the most serious proliferation threat in the world. They have been so for the past decade and a half. Since 1980, China has supplied billions of dollars' worth of nuclear weapons, chemical weapons and missile technology to South Asia, South Africa, South America and the Middle East. It has done so in the teeth of U.S. protests,

Reprinted from Gary Milhollin's statement before the United States Senate Committee on Foreign Relations, Washington, DC, October 8, 1997.

and despite repeated promises to stop. The exports are still going on, and while they do, they make it impossible for the United States and its allies to halt the spread of weapons of mass destruction. . . .

China has consistently undermined U.S. nonproliferation efforts for nearly two decades and is still doing so today.

Missiles and non-compliance

In the early 1990s, Chinese companies were caught selling Pakistan M-11 missile components. The M-11 is an accurate, solid-fuel missile that can carry a nuclear warhead about 300 kilometers. In June 1991, the Bush administration sanctioned the two offending Chinese sellers. The sanctions were supposed to last for at least two years, but they were waived less than a year later, in March 1992, when China promised to abide by the guidelines of the Missile Technology Control Regime, a multinational agreement to restrict missile sales.

But the sales continued and in August 1993, the Clinton administration applied sanctions again for two years, after determining that China had violated the U.S. missile sanctions law a second time. Then in October 1994, the United States lifted the sanctions early again, when China pledged once more to stop its missile sales and comply with the Missile Technology Control Regime.

China has consistently undermined U.S. nonproliferation efforts for nearly two decades and is still doing so today.

Since 1994, the stream of missile exports has continued. U.S. satellites and human intelligence have watched missile technicians travel back and forth between Beijing and Islamabad and have watched steady transfers of missile-related equipment. U.S. officials say that China's missile exports have continued up until the present moment, unabated.

In fact, our officials have learned that they were duped in 1992 and 1994. China was not promising what we thought it was. Our officials now realize that China interprets its promises in 1992 and 1994 so narrowly as to make them practically meaningless. It is clear that China has not complied with the Missile Technology Control Regime in the past, that it is not complying now, and that it probably never will comply unless something happens to change China's attitude on this question.

In addition to its sales to Pakistan, China has also sold Saudi Arabia medium-range, nuclear-capable missiles, and sold Iran missile guidance components. The intelligence community has completed an air-tight finding of fact that the missile sale to Iran happened. All the legal and factual analysis necessary to apply sanctions has been finished since last year, but the findings have lain dormant since then. The State Department has chosen not to complete the administrative process because if it did, it would have to apply sanctions and give up its engagement policy. The sanctions law is not achieving either deterrence or punishment, as Congress intended.

In its latest venture, China is helping to build a plant to produce M-11 missiles in Pakistan. [In 1998, Pakistan tested its first nuclear device.] U.S. officials say that activity at the plant is "very high." If the Chinese continue to help at their present rate, the plant could be ready for missile production within a year. This activity, combined with the State Department's refusal to apply sanctions to China, means that the United States is now giving a green light to one of the most dangerous missile plants in the world.

Poison gas

In addition to missiles, China has been selling the means to make poison gas. In 1995 I discovered, and wrote in the *New York Times*, that the United States had caught China exporting poison gas ingredients to Iran, and that the sales had been going on for at least three years. In 1996, the press reported that China was sending entire factories for making poison gas to Iran, including special glass-lined vessels for mixing precursor chemicals. The shipments also included 400 tons of chemicals useful for making nerve agents.

The result is that by now, in 1997, China has been outfitting Iran with ingredients and equipment to make poison gas for at least five years. U.S. officials say that the poison gas sales are continuing despite our government's decision in May 1997 to sanction five Chinese individuals and two companies for contributing to Iran's chemical weapons program.

Nuclear weapons

China has also been the leading proliferator of nuclear weapon technology in the world. China gave Pakistan nearly everything it needed to make its first atomic bomb. In the early 1980s, China gave Pakistan a tested nuclear weapon design and enough high-enriched uranium to fuel it. This has to be one of the most egregious acts of nuclear proliferation in history. Then, China helped Pakistan produce high-enriched uranium with gas centrifuges. More recently, it has helped Pakistan build a reactor to produce plutonium and tritium for nuclear weapons, and has helped Pakistan increase the number of its centrifuges so it can boost its production of high-enriched uranium.

China's most recent export was of specialized ring magnets, which are used in the suspension bearings of gas centrifuge rotors. The sale was revealed in early 1996. The magnets were shipped directly to a secret nuclear weapon production site in Pakistan, and were sent without requiring international inspection. The seller was a subsidiary of the China National Nuclear Corporation, an arm of the Chinese government. In my opinion, this export violated China's pledge under the Nuclear Nonproliferation Treaty, which it joined in 1992. Article III of the Treaty forbids the sale of such items without requiring international inspection. The sale also violated China's pledge under the Article I of the Treaty not to help other countries make nuclear weapons. Yet, the State Department has not sanctioned China for this sale, or even complained about it publicly.

There is also concern within the U.S. government that Pakistani scientists may be receiving nuclear weapon related information through their visits to the Chinese Academy of Engineering Physics. The Academy designs China's nuclear weapons.

Iran is the next candidate for China's nuclear help. The Beijing Research Institute of Uranium Geology (BRIUG) has been helping Iran prospect for uranium. . . . Any uranium it finds is likely to go directly into Iran's nuclear weapon program. This Institute is part of the China National Nuclear Corporation (CNNC). . . . China has apparently promised to stop this activity, but this promise, like China's other promises, must be treated with skepticism.

China has also been talking to Iran about selling a 25 to 30 megawatt nuclear reactor, which is an ideal size for making a few nuclear weapons per year. Also on the horizon is a plant to produce uranium hexafluoride from uranium concentrate, a step necessary to enrich uranium for use in atomic bombs.

These latter two sales are being held over our heads like swords. If we don't start cooperating more with China in the nuclear area, then China will complete these two dangerous export deals with Iran. This amounts to nuclear blackmail.

China has . . . been the leading proliferator of nuclear weapon technology in the world.

The conclusion has to be that our engagement policy toward China has failed. The policy is not producing any change in China's behavior, nor even producing engagement. The negotiation process is effectively dead. The Chinese are not even talking to us about their chemical and missile exports. We are simply watching the Chinese shipments go out, without any hope of stopping them. All our present policy has produced is a new missile factory in Pakistan, an upgraded nuclear weapon factory in Pakistan and new chemical weapon plants in Iran. In time, it will probably produce a nuclear weapon factory in Iran.

This failure will be compounded if the United States begins nuclear trade with China without stopping these exports. If we sell China nuclear reactors while China is still selling missiles and poison gas ingredients to Iran and Pakistan, what will we be saying to the world? The message will be that no matter how bad China's exports are, we still can't resist making a buck from our own exports. No wonder China doesn't take us seriously. The United States should not begin exporting nuclear technology to China until China stops exporting mass destruction technology to other countries. It would be folly to "de-link" nuclear proliferation from other forms of proliferation.

Buying from America and exporting to Iran

There is considerable evidence that American technology may be fueling some of these dangerous Chinese exports. I have listed two cases where this appears to have happened. There are undoubtedly others.

Case 41: The C-801 and C-802 Anti-Ship Missiles.

Iran recently bought these new anti-ship missiles from the China Precision Machinery Import-Export Corporation (CPMIEC). Admiral John Redd, our naval commander in the Persian Gulf, took the unusual step of complaining publicly about the sale. Iran appears to have up to 60 of these missiles so far, plus fast attack boats to carry them. The missiles are a threat to our ships and sailors in the Gulf and they are also a threat to commercial shipping.

It seems quite likely that these missiles were built with help from the United States. . . . The sensitive, controlled equipment that the U.S. Commerce Department approved for export to China Precision Machinery from 1989 to 1993 [includes] computer workstations for the simulation of wind effects, flight data recorders, and navigational instruments. The ability to simulate wind effects is something the designer of an anti-ship missile could find quite useful. I would like to emphasize that all of this equipment was deemed so sensitive that it required an individual validated export license to leave the United States.

[The Risk Report that my project publishes] lists the companies around the world that are suspected of contributing to the proliferation of weapons of mass destruction. It includes China Precision Machinery Import-Export Corporation, which was sanctioned in 1993 by the United States for exporting missile components to Pakistan.

If the question is: Who has been helping Iran build anti-ship missiles to threaten our sailors? The answer may well be: The U.S. Commerce Department.

Case 42: Air Surveillance Radar.

Iran recently imported a powerful surveillance radar from the China National Electronics Import-Export Corporation. The radar is now part of Iran's air defense system, and it can detect targets up to 300 kilometers away. If the United States ever comes to blows with Iran, American pilots will have to contend with it.

If we don't start cooperating more with China in the nuclear area, then China will complete . . . two dangerous export deals with Iran. This amounts to nuclear blackmail.

This radar too seems to have been built with help from the United States. . . . Sensitive, controlled equipment that the U.S. Commerce Department approved for export to China National Electronics from 1989 to 1993 totals $9.7 million. It includes things like equipment for microwave research, a very large scale integrated system for testing integrated circuits, equipment for making semiconductors, and a shipment of computer gear worth $4.3 million. All of this equipment appears highly useful for developing radar, and all of it was deemed so sensitive that it required an individual validated export license to leave the United States.

If the question is: Who has been helping Iran build air defenses? The answer may well be: The U.S. Commerce Department.

I would like to point out that in these two cases, the exports were approved under the Bush Administration. I urge the Committee to obtain and study the exports approved under the Clinton Administration. The generally pro-export stance of the Clinton Administration leads one to suspect that China is importing even more sensitive high-technology from the United States today. I cannot emphasize too strongly the need for effective Congressional oversight of our export licensing process. The lack of Congressional oversight was one of the main reasons why the Commerce Department approved so many sensitive American exports to Iraq before the Gulf War.

In addition to these two cases, other Chinese organizations involved in military or nuclear weapon work have either received sensitive American products or may do so soon.

A fusion reactor

In 1993–94, the Institute of Plasma Physics of the Chinese Academy of Sciences transferred a nuclear fusion research reactor to the Azad University in Tehran. The reactor is a training device ostensibly used for peaceful purposes. Despite this help to Iran, and despite being a well-known contributor to China's nuclear and missile programs, the Academy of Sciences managed recently to import an American super-computer from Silicon Graphics, Inc.

So if the question is: What happens to a Chinese organization that helps Iran do nuclear research? The answer is: It can import an American supercomputer.

Uranium exploration

I have mentioned above the uranium prospecting in Iran by the China National Nuclear Corporation (CNNC). The CNNC has been implicated in the sale of ring magnets to the A. Q. Khan Research Laboratory in Pakistan, which enriches uranium for nuclear weapons, and it is also involved in the development of Pakistan's secret nuclear reactor at Khusab. A CNNC subsidiary is currently constructing a power reactor for Pakistan at Chashma. CNNC would be the key player in any nuclear cooperation agreement that might be implemented between the United States and China. Right now, our government, under pressure from Westinghouse, is planning to revive the cooperation agreement that has been stalled since 1984 because of China's bad proliferation behavior.

If the question is: What happens to a Chinese organization that helps Iran prospect for uranium and helps Pakistan make nuclear weapons? The answer is: The United States government tries to find a way to sell it American nuclear technology.

None of these Chinese missile, nuclear and military organizations is on the Commerce Department's list of dangerous buyers. American exporters are free to sell these companies sensitive dual use equipment as long as the equipment is not on the small list of items that are still controlled for export. These organizations could get a high-speed American computer—performing up to two billion operations per second—without an export license, or in some cases up to seven billion if the exporter could claim that it did not know what the buyer was up to.

The names of these four organizations should be added to the Commerce Department's list immediately. So should several others such as

China North Industries Corporation (Norinco). Its Hong Kong subsidiary was shut down in July by the Hong Kong government for smuggling materials to make poison gas to Iran, and in 1996 its employees were indicted for conspiring to import 2,000 automatic weapons into California for street gangs.

I urge this Committee to ask the U.S. intelligence agencies why these companies have not been listed. I am convinced that our government—and in particular our intelligence agencies—should be doing more to help exporters avoid dangerous sales.

Diverting American equipment

On July 1, the press reported that yet another sensitive American export had been diverted in China. A super-computer manufactured by Sun Microsystems of Mountain View, California had wound up at China's National University of Defense Technology in Changsha. The University, which is run by the People's Liberation Army, does research and training in advanced weapons systems. It specializes in missile design, detonation physics, super-computer development, and automatic target recognition. Scientists at Changsha plan to develop the next generation of Chinese weapons with American equipment.

In September 1997, our government announced that China had agreed to return the super-computer. The Commerce Department claimed that this result was a victory, and that it was due to a safeguards system that the United States has in place for preventing diversions.

In fact, the United States has no such system. China's diversion was a defeat for the Administration, and the decision to return the super-computer was a victory for Congress.

China intentionally committed fraud to get the [tools to build the B-1 strategic bomber].

The diversion of the Sun super-computer was discovered only after Congress demanded an investigation to find out what had happened to the many American super-computers that had been exported since early 1996, when the Administration slashed export controls. To satisfy Congress, the Commerce Department asked Sun Microsystems about its exports. Only then did Sun disclose the diversion. If Congress had not forced the Commerce Department to conduct an investigation, the Sun super-computer would still be in China, helping to design advanced weapons.

The Sun diversion is not an isolated case. In 1994, China wanted to import sensitive American machine tools that had been used to build the B-1 strategic bomber. To do so, China promised the U.S. government that the machines would be used to make civilian aircraft in Beijing. Instead, the machines were diverted immediately to a missile and military aircraft factory in Nanchang. Satellite photos have since revealed that at the very time the Chinese were promising to use the machines in Beijing, the Chinese were constructing a special building in Nanchang to house one of the largest ones, a stretch press. China intentionally committed fraud to get the equipment.

The Commerce Department now admits that China has imported at least 47 American super-computers since early 1996 without export licenses. The press reports that the real figure is much higher. These imports were made possible by the Clinton Administration's decision in late 1995 to slash export controls. The Chinese Academy of Sciences, which helps develop China's nuclear weapons and long-range missiles, bought a super-computer from Silicon Graphics, Inc. that performs approximately six billion operations per second.

According to Chinese government publications, the Academy of Sciences oversees institutes that perform missile and military research as well as research related to nuclear weapons. In the 1970s, the Academy helped develop the flight computer for the DF-5 intercontinental missile, which can target U.S. cities with nuclear warheads. The Academy's Mechanics Institute has developed advanced rocket propellant and helped develop the shield for the warhead of China's first ICBM. The Academy's Institute of Electronics has built synthetic aperture radar useful in military mapping and surveillance, and its Acoustic Institute has developed a guidance system for the Yu-3 torpedo, together with sonar for nuclear and conventional submarines.

In the nuclear field, the Academy has developed separation membranes to enrich uranium by gaseous diffusion, and its Institute of Mechanics has studied the effects of underground nuclear weapon tests and ways to protect against nuclear explosions. It has also studied the stability of plasma in controlled nuclear fusion. Its Institute of Electronics has developed various kinds of lasers used in atomic isotope separation.

According to information published by Silicon Graphics, the super-computer it sold to the Academy is now the "most powerful SNIP super-computer in China," and provides China "computational power previously unknown." According to information that I have received from industry sources, the most powerful computers previously sold to China operated at approximately 1.5 billion operations per second. If this information is accurate, the Silicon Graphics machine is roughly four times more powerful than anything China had before.

The new computer, which was financed by a loan from the World Bank, has become the centerpiece of the Academy's new Computer Network Information Center. According to the Academy, the computer is now available to "all the major scientific and technological institutes across China." This means that any Chinese organization that is designing nuclear weapons or long-range missiles has access to it. In effect, Chinese weapon designers can use the Silicon Graphics machines to design lighter nuclear warheads to fit on longer-range and more accurate missiles capable of reaching U.S. cities. This is a giant loss for U.S. security.

Nuclear cooperation between the United States and China

Chinese President Jiang Zemin is scheduled to visit the United States at the end of October 1997. In preparation for this event, the Clinton Administration is planning to certify that China has stopped helping other countries develop nuclear weapons. This certification, which no other

American president has been willing to make for the past 12 years, would open the door for U.S. companies such as Westinghouse to sell China nuclear reactors.

The certification is based on a statement on May 11, 1996, by an unidentified spokesman for the Chinese Foreign Ministry in response to a reporter's question. The spokesman said that "China will not provide assistance to unsafeguarded nuclear facilities." The Administration contends that China has not broken that promise for the past 16 months, and therefore, China has stopped helping other countries develop nuclear weapons.

Chinese weapon designers can use the [U.S.-made] Silicon Graphics machines to design lighter nuclear warheads to fit on longer-range and more accurate missiles capable of reaching the U.S.

First, there is the factual question: Is this true? I recommend that the Committee get a briefing from the intelligence agencies describing all of China's nuclear aid to other countries since May 1996. The briefing should include information on whether China is still helping Iran prospect for uranium, and whether Pakistani scientists are receiving nuclear weapon related technology through visits to Chinese nuclear weapon sites.

Second, is the promise adequate? China is only promising not to aid facilities; it will remain free to aid programs. Pakistan's program has unsafeguarded facilities that are producing nuclear weapons. China will continue to aid that program, and China's aid will inevitably spill over into bomb-making. An atom cannot tell whether it is military or civilian.

China, in fact, is the only nuclear supplier country that refuses to require full-scope safeguards on its exports. Full-scope means requiring that all of a country's facilities be under international inspection, which would bar aid to countries like Pakistan. In effect, China is trying to reap the benefits of nuclear trade without shouldering the burdens. With one hand, China wants to import American nuclear technology. With the other, it wants to help Pakistan's nuclear bomb program. China should be required to make a choice. If China wants nuclear trade with the United States, it can give up nuclear trade with Pakistan. That is the only deal the United States should be willing to make.

10

India and Pakistan Threaten Nuclear Security

Steven Lee Myers

Steven Lee Myers is a reporter for the New York Times. *He frequently writes about events in Southeast Asia.*

Nuclear tests by India and Pakistan in 1998 have made the possibility of nuclear war more likely. The two countries share a disputed border and have engaged in three wars against one another. Should either India or Pakistan develop the technology to deploy its nuclear weapons, they are unlikely to exercise the restraint and caution that the United States and the former Soviet Union did during the Cold War. Furthermore, China—Pakistan's ally and one of the five nuclear powers—could be pulled into the conflict, and the stability of Southeast Asia could be destroyed.

On their northern border, high in the Himalayas, India and Pakistan have for years been fighting for position and not much else along a glacier that is virtually uninhabitable. On mountains reaching 20,000 feet, their armies snipe and trade artillery blasts, if the weather allows. By most definitions, it is war, but a small war. Each side loses as many soldiers to altitude sickness as to combat.

The May 1998 nuclear tests by Pakistan—coming two weeks after India's own tests—have abruptly and fundamentally changed the confrontation between India and Pakistan, which had become a limited, relatively low-intensity military standoff.

Although both countries have had covert nuclear programs for decades, the tests brought both much closer to actually putting nuclear weapons in their arsenals and, worse, on the potential battlefields along their hotly disputed border.

That is why arms-control experts say the truly alarming thing that Pakistan's Prime Minister Nawaz Sharif's Government announced was not that Pakistan had successfully conducted its own tests. Rather it was the declaration that Pakistan was already fitting nuclear warheads on top of a missile, tested only last month, that is capable of striking most of India.

Michael Krepon, the president of the Henry L. Stimson Center, an independent research institute in Washington, D.C., said the development of nuclear weapons progressed in clear stages: from research to design to tests to the making of the bombs or warheads themselves.

"A crucial threshold has been crossed, if it's true," Mr. Krepon said of Pakistan's declaration about fitting its missile. "And that means we have only two thresholds left: deployment and use."

Testing is far from using

For all the rhetorical bluster by both sides, though, there is still a large gap between conducting successful tests and building effective, usable weapons. And that is where officials in Washington and around the world are looking these days for a glimmer of hope that there is still time to head off a terrifying spiral of escalation that could draw in India's other enemy, China.

India is said to have enough fissile material for perhaps 50 nuclear devices, maybe more. Pakistan has enough for perhaps 12. Experts have long assumed that both can make Hiroshima-scale bombs to drop from planes, but that is considered an unreliable way to deliver nuclear weapons since planes can be shot down.

There is almost no evidence that either country has mastered the ability to make warheads small enough to fit on missiles, though not for lack of trying. Senior Administration officials cast doubt on Pakistan's claims to have already fitted its longest-range missile with nuclear warheads. "That would be a fateful and foolish step," one official said on condition of anonymity.

Even so, the mere claim was sure to leave India's nuclear strategists wondering, intensifying already inflamed emotions. And the experts agreed it is only a matter of time before both can field nuclear warheads.

In recent years both India and Pakistan have come to rely more and more on their strategic forces. Pakistan, in particular, has poured its scarce resources into developing nuclear weapons and ballistic missiles, purchasing equipment and technology from China, as well as North Korea. (More than a quarter of Pakistan's federal spending goes to defense, compared to 14 percent for India.)

Nuclear tests by Pakistan—coming two weeks after India's own tests—have abruptly and fundamentally changed the confrontation between India and Pakistan.

Pakistan has taken this route to compensate for an overwhelming disadvantage in conventional forces. India has twice as many soldiers— nearly 1.2 million to about 600,000—and twice as many combat aircraft. What's more, much of Pakistan's population and economic heart lie within easy striking distance of India's border, leaving it vulnerable.

While Pakistan has a number of short-range missiles, it tested its first longer-range missile in April 1999, a test that India cited as provocation when it conducted its nuclear tests. Pakistan's missile is said to have a range of 900 miles, which would bring most of India's major cities within striking distance. Although built with North Korean help, Pakistan named it the Ghauri, after a Muslim warrior who defeated a 12th-century Hindu ruler of India named Prithvi.

While Pakistan lags behind India in conventional forces, many experts say it may have an edge in missiles. India's most effective missiles, the Prithvi series, have relatively short ranges. And while India has tested a longer-ranged missile, called the Agni, it has yet to complete its development.

Interventional concerns

In the meantime, the United States and other countries are scrambling to stop South Asia's suddenly revived arms race before it escalates any further. On Friday [May 1998], the United Nations Security Council called on India and Pakistan to sign the treaties against the spread and testing of nuclear weapons that, until now, had limited the world's declared nuclear powers to the United States, Russia, Britain, France and China.

The hope is that India and Pakistan will call a halt to their nuclear programs where they now stand, although neither has so far shown much willingness to heed the world's pleas. The Pakistanis "are ready to die for their respect," Mr. Sharif warned in a televised address to his nation, brushing aside the sanctions the United States imposed only hours later.

The world could be closer to nuclear war than at any time since the Cuban missile crisis in 1962.

For now, the best hope may lie with the fact that a fundamental taboo has existed against the use of nuclear weapons ever since the world learned what those weapons could do when the United States dropped them on Japan to end World War II. That and the prospect of "mutually assured destruction," known widely by the grim acronym MAD, kept the United States and Soviet Union from firing them throughout the cold war.

But India and Pakistan have suddenly made the specter of a nuclear exchange seem less remote. The United States and the Soviet Union, after all, never shared a border. Nor did they directly quarrel over a territory as volatile as Jammu and Kashmir, the predominantly Muslim enclave carved up after India and Pakistan gained independence from Britain in 1947.

"Unresolved disagreements, deep animosity and distrust, and the continuing confrontation between their forces in disputed Kashmir make the subcontinent region with a significant risk of nuclear confrontation," the Pentagon concluded in a report published before May 1999's tit-for-tat tests.

Arms-control experts now worry that the world could be closer to nuclear war than at any time since the Cuban missile crisis in 1962 [when the United States and the former Soviet Union nearly exchanged nuclear fire]. That was the only time in the 53 years of the nuclear age when it seemed likely that any two nuclear powers might descend into direct large-scale hostilities with each other. American and Chinese troops fought in the Korean War, but that was long before China had nuclear weapons; China and India fought a border war in 1962, but that was before either went nuclear.

In those same 53 years, India and Pakistan have fought three wars and have perpetually seemed on the verge of a fourth—never with more devastating potential consequences than now.

11

U.S. Allies in the Mideast Threaten Nuclear Security

Amy Dockser Marcus

Amy Dockser Marcus is a staff reporter for the Wall Street Journal.

The United States now faces as much danger from its Middle Eastern allies such as Israel and Syria as it does from its enemies such as Iran and Iraq. Allies frequently obtain nuclear weapon-making knowledge and technology from Western countries and pass them on to other Mideastern nations that are hostile to the United States. When the United States applies pressure on its allies to stop the proliferation of nuclear weapons technology, however, the allies simply continue the proliferation clandestinely. Historically, the United States condoned efforts by its allies in the Mideast to develop nuclear weapons, but that policy has led to increased international danger of nuclear proliferation.

Addressing a congressional panel earlier in 1996, CIA Director John Deutch called proliferation of biological, chemical and nuclear weapons the main strategic threat facing the U.S. and its allies. The big danger lies in the Mideast, he added, as so-called rogue states such as Iran, Iraq and Libya seek to acquire such weapons.

With unconventional weapons, "the potential for surprise is greater than it was in the days when we could focus our energies on the well-recognized instruments of Soviet power," Mr. Deutch warned.

But for U.S. policy makers, the biggest surprise of all may be that the next Mideast proliferation crisis is just as likely to involve U.S. allies as the rogue states.

Egypt recently resumed efforts to acquire long-range ballistic missiles and is stepping up research in chemical and biological weapons. Israel is believed to be developing missiles that can reach as far as the former Soviet Union, an achievement that military analysts say could alter the regional balance of power. Even American allies in the Persian Gulf that are largely dependent on the U.S. for security, such as Saudi Arabia and the United Arab Emirates, have acquired ballistic missiles capable of carrying conventional and unconventional warheads.

Syria's missile tests

And Syria, considered a U.S. partner to the degree that it is participating in the American-sponsored peace talks, has just conducted a third test of an extended-range Scud-C missile, and its chemical-weapons program is the most advanced in the Arab world, surpassing even Iraq's.

No one says the leaders of longstanding allies such as Egypt, Israel and Saudi Arabia should now be put in the same category as perennial trouble-makers such as Libya's Moammar Gadhafi or Iraq's Saddam Hussein. The Iraqi army's attack on the Kurdish city of Arbil in northern Iraq in September 1996 prompted a U.S. military response and demonstrated that Saddam Hussein still threatens regional stability. Contentions by United Nations officials that Iraq continues to hide the extent of its unconventional-weapons program and recent reports that Iran is developing biological weapons potentially as lethal as a nuclear strike are also worrisome.

Yet amid America's relentless drive to isolate countries it perceives as its enemies, the growing problem with allies is being overlooked. "How do you deal with friends who have developed nasty capabilities?" asks Michael Eisenstadt, a Mideast military-affairs analyst at the Washington Institute for Near East Policy.

Going easy on friends

Until recently, answering that question wasn't urgent. The U.S. quietly tolerated unconventional-weapons plans in friends that it loudly protested in enemies. U.S. policy was based partly on the idea that it couldn't push for arms reduction among allies while coaxing them to join peace negotiations. For years, some military analysts even contended that efforts by Egypt, Israel and, to a lesser extent, Syria to develop unconventional weapons might tend to stabilize the Mideast by helping deter military confrontations.

But no longer. The entire Mideast is infected with "creeping proliferation," says Anthony Cordesman, a senior fellow at the Center for Strategic and International Studies in Washington. Advances in technology are enabling all the countries to increase their capability to deliver, even if crudely, unconventional weapons over long distances. "It is virtually impossible any longer to separate what's happening in the Iran and Iraq arena from developments in countries that are the U.S.'s closest regional allies," Mr. Cordesman says.

The lines are blurring as cooperation between U.S. allies and rogue states in the development, transfer and even funding of unconventional weapons intensifies. Central Intelligence Agency Director John Deutch's congressional testimony focused on Iran's growing arsenal but ignored the virtual strategic cooperation between Syria and Iran in developing biological and chemical weapons. The two countries shared the costs of setting up domestic plants to produce North Korean Scud-C missiles and apparently chemical warheads, according to Dany Shoham, a former Israeli intelligence officer who now studies unconventional warfare at the Besa Center for Strategic Studies at Bar-Ilan University in Tel Aviv.

Extensive ties

Syria and Iran ship and exchange missile parts, transfer information on new technology, and are believed to exchange technicians and specialists in unconventional weapons, according to Mr. Shoham and U.S. military analysts. They are also believed to be helping finance the development of North Korea's long-range Nodong I missile, which both Mideastern countries are interested in acquiring.

Such cooperation is difficult to stop, says Jean Pascal Zanders, a proliferation expert at the Center for Peace Research in the Free University of Brussels. "The countries often present their unconventional-weapons programs as part of the Arab national cause," he says. "They get assistance from Arab scientists in various countries who are attracted either by good pay or pan-Arab nationalistic sentiments."

For U.S. policy makers, the biggest surprise of all may be that the next Mideast proliferation crisis is just as likely to involve U.S. allies as the rogue states.

That can occur even between countries with low-level diplomatic relations. Egypt sided with the U.S.-led coalition against Iraq in the 1991 Gulf War, but over the past year Egyptian scientists who went home during the fighting have quietly returned to Iraq's military industries, Israeli and U.S. experts say. A delegation from the U.N. commission monitoring the dismantling of Iraq's unconventional-weapons program went to Cairo in 1995 seeking information about Egyptian-Iraqi cooperation on missile development before the Gulf War and about Iraq's current weapons arsenal but was rebuffed by Egyptian officials, informed people say. The U.N. declines to comment.

But the most important way that U.S. allies in the region help rogue states is through their willingness to trade or sell information they gain through access to European and U.S. academic institutions, participation in international conferences on technology, and greater ability to obtain "dual use" technologies applicable in civilian and military industries alike.

"A country like Egypt has access to a whole range of things around the world that are simply not available to countries that are outcasts," says Joseph Bermudez Jr., a New York military-affairs analyst specializing in proliferation issues.

Limited success

U.S. pressure, even on allies such as Egypt and Israel that get a lot of U.S. aid, has had limited success. Mr. Bermudez, an expert in North Korean military affairs, says Israel offered to invest in North Korea's civilian industry if Pyongyang would agree not to transfer its Nodong I missile to Iran. After Washington objected, Israel suspended the initiative, but Mr.

Bermudez notes widespread speculation that Israel is still quietly trying to influence North Korea. U.S. efforts to persuade Egypt to take an active role in curbing proliferation of North Korean weapons failed, mainly because North Korea remains a major supplier to Egypt, Mr. Bermudez says.

In other instances, the U.S. has avoided applying much pressure. Regional arms-control talks being conducted as part of the Arab-Israeli peace negotiations have been frozen for 18 months, but the U.S. hasn't tried seriously enough to get the various sides back to the table, says Bruce W. Jentleson, a former member of the U.S. delegation and now director of a Washington research center run by the University of California at Davis. And even though U.S. analysts estimate that Israel has developed as many as 200 nuclear warheads, a number far surpassing its defense needs, U.S. pressure on Israel about its nuclear capabilities has been minimal, Israeli and U.S. military analysts agree.

It is virtually impossible any longer to separate what's happening in the Iran and Iraq arena from developments in countries that are the U.S.'s closest regional allies.

In the future, moreover, U.S. ability to exert pressure is likely to dwindle. Most Mideastern countries, whether U.S. allies or not, either deny that they maintain unconventional-weapons programs or simply refuse to talk about them. And gathering intelligence about such programs is getting harder. The Washington Institute's Mr. Eisenstadt says biological weapons, though potentially as destructive as nuclear arms, are hard to detect. Militarily useful quantities can be produced with off-the-shelf equipment found in pharmaceuticals companies and can be easily hidden because the work can be done in a small room. Even nuclear programs are getting easier to conceal, with the collapse of the former Soviet Union leading to potentially greater availability of fissionable material that could make construction of huge production facilities unnecessary.

Special zone discussed

Many of the players—allies and rogues alike—say the only solution is to create a regional zone free of weapons of mass destruction, but progress has been slow. Israel and Jordan signed a treaty calling for the two countries to work toward establishing such a zone, but "we haven't even actually agreed yet on a definition of what constitutes the Middle East region," says Mohammad Khair Shiyyab, who heads the Department of Security Studies at the University of Jordan in Amman.

Ahmed Fakhr, director of the National Center for Middle East Studies in Cairo, says the U.S. must end what he calls its "double standard" in addressing the issue of unconventional weapons in the Mideast. "The U.S. is willing to focus on the threat from the potential nuclear capability of an Iran or an Iraq but turns a blind eye to Israel's nuclear program," says Mr. Fakhr, who served on Egypt's delegation to the regional arms-control talks.

The U.S. policy, which is indeed based on willingness to cut its regional allies some slack, seems to be in trouble. Intelligence reports leaked to the news media earlier in 1996 cited worry about growing domestic instability in Egypt and the dangers—given the size of the country's missile arsenal—if a government hostile to the U.S. came to power.

Toward Syria, U.S. policy is shaped by the perception that Syrian President Hafez Assad, unlike Iraq's Saddam Hussein, "isn't an adventurer," says one U.S. intelligence official, but that notion may become irrelevant. Some analysts say Syria might use chemical or biological weapons covertly, in a way that could not be tied to it directly.

Israel also poses potential trouble. Because recent technological advances might facilitate a limited unconventional attack that could impede Israel's ability to defend itself, the Israeli government might make a harsh pre-emptive or retaliatory strike even if the country's existence isn't immediately threatened, some analysts say.

Such dangers, they add, may soon force the U.S. to reconsider the political tradeoffs that it once willingly made when dealing with allies on the weapons issue.

"In the current geopolitical constellation of today's Middle East, it's still possible to argue that Iran, Iraq and the other rogue states pose the greatest security threat," Mr. Shoham says. "But the political situation in the region is so fragile, and unconventional weapons capabilities are developing so quickly, that in less than five years there's going to be no real difference in terms of the level of potential threat from an Iran or an Iraq than there is from a Syria, Libya, Egypt, Algeria or any other place in the Middle East."

12

The United States Is a Threat to Nuclear Security

M.V. Ramana

M.V. Ramana is a research associate at the Center for Energy and Environmental Studies at Princeton University, in Princeton, New Jersey.

The United States hypocritically demands that countries without nuclear arms refrain from developing them while it retains its own nuclear arsenals in spite of increasing national and international protest and in violation of numerous treaties. Efforts by the United States to maintain its nuclear arsenal seriously threaten global security by encouraging countries to develop nuclear arms in order to protect themselves against established nuclear threats. Growing proliferation of nuclear weapons increases the likelihood that some nation will accidentally or intentionally deploy a nuclear bomb at another country; such a deployment would likely be answered with nuclear force and could set off a global nuclear war.

The nuclear tests by India and Pakistan in May 1998 were a reminder to the world that the dangers posed by nuclear weapons are still very much with us. Most of the analyses that followed these tests paid little attention to the nuclear weapons states and their reluctance to keep up their commitments under the Nuclear Non-Proliferation Treaty that came into force in 1970.[1] Throughout its nuclear history, India has repeatedly pointed out the inequity of the international arrangement—nuclear apartheid, as some Indian commentators have termed it. This arrangement allows some nations to possess hugely destructive nuclear arsenals, while other nations are denied that choice.[2]

On May 28, 1998, following the first set of nuclear tests by Pakistan, President Bill Clinton said, "I cannot believe that we are about to start the 21st century by having the Indian subcontinent repeat the worst mistakes of the 20th century, when we know it is not necessary to peace, to security, to prosperity, to national greatness or personal fulfillment."[3] This is perhaps the closest a president of the United States has come to officially stating, albeit grudgingly, that nuclear weapons are not necessary for

Reprinted with permission from "Reinventing the Arms Race," by M.V. Ramana, *Forum for Applied Research & Public Policy*, Summer 1999.

peace or security. Actions taken by the United States send out a different message, however, and recent decisions taken by the administration and the U.S. Department of Energy [DOE] indicate that the U.S. leadership intends to keep its nuclear arsenal around for the foreseeable future and thereby to perpetuate the arms race.

At the same time, a number of initiatives in the international arena, as well as recommendations by various national and international bodies, advocate the elimination—or at least rapid reductions in numbers—of nuclear weapons. If serious steps are not taken towards abolition of nuclear weapons, this growing polarization between the nuclear weapons states and the vast majority of nonnuclear countries could lead to unraveling of the current international regime, which may have dire consequences.

After the CTBT

The long-sought Comprehensive Test Ban Treaty, signed by President Clinton in 1996, was the first major nuclear agreement negotiated after the Cold War. In the preamble to the treaty, the signatories—including 152 nonnuclear states and the five nuclear weapon states [United States, Russia, China, England, and France]—declared that they intended to take effective measures towards nuclear disarmament. They stressed the need for continued systematic and progressive efforts to reduce nuclear weapons worldwide, with the ultimate goal of eliminating those weapons. Most of the countries that joined the treaty believed it would indeed hasten elimination. But Stephen Ledogar, the U.S. ambassador to the Comprehensive Test Ban Treaty negotiations, revealed a different picture about the beliefs of the nuclear weapons states. While most countries believe banning nuclear tests will by itself reduce nuclear weapons stockpiles, "all five nuclear weapons states believe that without testing, we can nevertheless maintain for the foreseeable future the viability, the safety and the reliability of our nuclear stockpiles."[4]

Stockpile stewardship

The safety and reliability of the U.S. arsenal are to be maintained through a multi-billion dollar program called the "Science Based Stockpile Stewardship" program. Stockpile Stewardship is seen by many as a way of buying off the nuclear weapons laboratories to get their consent to the United States signing the Comprehensive Test Ban Treaty. By retaining "all historical capabilities of the weapons laboratories, industrial plants and the Nevada Test Site," Stockpile Stewardship will provide design capabilities potentially greater than during the Cold War.[5]

The plan calls for maintaining weapons, weapons components, and research and development facilities such as Los Alamos and Lawrence Livermore National Laboratories and the Nevada Test Site. Stockpile Stewardship also supports a National Ignition Facility that attempts to achieve nuclear fusion. Critics have raised questions about potential uses of this facility to develop new pure-fusion weapons. In addition, the Department of Energy plans to spend more than $1 billion at Los Alamos to expand facilities for producing substantial numbers of nuclear warheads.[6] In addition to DOE's new, high-tech, experimental laboratory facilities, Stockpile Stewardship will use high-powered supercomputers to conduct virtual tests or simulate nuclear explosions.[7] Over the next decade, the United States plans to invest $45 billion in this program—an amount, in inflation-adjusted dollars, well above the average Cold War annual spending for nuclear weapons research, development, and testing.

Obviously, DOE plans go significantly beyond maintaining the safety and reliability of the arsenal. Barely a few months after President Bill Clinton signed the Test Ban Treaty, a legal petition by a coalition of nongovernmental organizations forced the release of a secret document which revealed that the weapons labs were currently working on "programs that provide new or modified designs."[8] Soon thereafter, DOE revealed its plans for the B61-11, a modification of an older nuclear gravity bomb. There are other new nuclear weapons under development as well.

These activities clearly show that even if the United States is complying with the letter of the test-ban treaty by not conducting full-scale nuclear explosions, it violates the spirit of the treaty. But that is not all. One reason India cited in refusing to sign the treaty was that the treaty no longer constrained development of nuclear weapons by the United States and other nuclear weapons states.[9] Thus U.S. policies actually have the perverse effect of strengthening arguments by other states in their quest for nuclear weapons.

Presidential directive

Instead of a reduced role for nuclear weapons, military planners have actually come up with new roles for these weapons despite the collapse of the Soviet Union nearly a decade ago. The Presidential Decision Directive 60, signed by President Bill Clinton in December 1997, allows such planning to continue. Far from backing a commitment to nuclear disarmament, this directive instead reaffirms the fundamental elements of U.S. nuclear doctrine since World War II. According to newspaper accounts, this directive recommits the United States to policies of threatened first use and threatened massive retaliation and affirms that the United States will continue to rely on nuclear arms as a cornerstone of its national security for the "indefinite future."[10] In addition, the presidential directive reportedly suggests the possibility of nuclear retaliation against countries suspected of possessing or manufacturing chemical and biological arms.[11] This conflicts directly with a U.S. pledge first initiated during the Carter administration in June 1978, and reaffirmed during the extension of the Nuclear Non-Proliferation Treaty in 1995. This pledge committed the nation to not using nuclear weapons against nonnuclear weapon states that are parties to the nonproliferation treaty.

START and stall

Some have charged that the nuclear weapons states are not really engaged in nuclear disarmament. In response, the United States and Russia have pointed to their bilateral negotiations aimed at limiting and reducing strategic armaments—the Strategic Arms Reduction Treaties (START). In 1991, the START I treaty, signed by the United States and Russia, limited the number of deployed strategic weapons to 6,000 each. This was further limited to 3,500 weapons each by the 1993 START II treaty. Both countries have signed the latter treaty, but only the United States has ratified it.

Now, nearly a decade later, the START process appears to have come to a stop. The Russian parliament, the Duma, refuses to ratify START II, in part because of the U.S. decision to open NATO to new members. Since the United States refuses to move forward unilaterally on START III, it seems highly unlikely that the START process will further reduce the numbers of nuclear weapons any time in the near future.

Shell game

What then has the START process achieved? First of all, it must be emphasized that in counting warheads that remain after the implementation of the START process, the numbers refer only to active operational weapons. But the U.S. Department of Defense [DOD] has spares in its stockpile, besides active operational warheads, kept at the bases where nuclear weapons are deployed. Further, DOD also holds separately a contingency stockpile, the augmentation or "hedge" warheads—that is, extra weapons available for redeployment. In addition, DOD has in storage reliability replacements—a third set of additional warheads maintained to replace those in the active arsenal in case those weapons prove faulty or unreliable. In addition to these stores, DOE has custody of retired warheads and the "strategic reserve"—more warheads not counted in the other categories. All these add up to over 10,000 warheads that are not counted under START. Russia also keeps several thousand warheads on reserve. It has been estimated that the United States and Russia together still have over 30,000 weapons. In all, the five nuclear weapons states hold between them over 36,000 weapons.[12]

Some nations . . . possess hugely destructive nuclear arsenals, while other nations are denied that choice.

Further, many of the components recovered from dismantled warheads—in particular the radioactive plutonium weapons parts, or pits as they are called, that provide the explosive capability to nuclear weapons—are mostly stored at the Pantex facility in Texas.[13] The only plans for disassembly are at the experimental, planning stage and would deal with only a few hundred pits. A decision about when and where to construct a full-scale pit disassembly plant has not yet been made.

By retaining these components of a large arsenal, the United States and Russia do not seem to be in any hurry to give up the potential to build up their arsenals. With the collapse of Russia's economy, there is also the danger that this large store of weapons materials may be diverted to other users.

The failure of the United States to pursue meaningful steps has been neatly summarized by a former director of Strategic and Theater Nuclear Weapons:

Those responsible for U.S. nuclear weapons must not lose

sight of the fact that the intent of these negotiations is not
to disarm the United States . . . the intent of U.S. arms negotiators is to disarm others, and experience demonstrates
that the disarmament of others is facilitated if U.S. weapons
are offered as compensation. Thus, we must have weapons
to give up.[14]

Ballistic missile defense

Russian opposition to ratifying START II is also fortified by recent steps
taken by the Clinton administration towards deploying a national missile
defense system. The system is ostensibly intended to shoot down missiles
launched at the United States. But scientists and analysts have long
pointed out the technical difficulties involved in constructing such a system and have demonstrated that even the best systems can be easily over-
whelmed by simple countermeasures. Nevertheless, the administration
has now allocated more than $10 billion over the next six years to field a
ballistic missile defense system by 2005, on top of the $55 billion spent
since 1983.

Despite this immense expenditure, current ballistic missile defense
systems have not been able to perform satisfactorily in tests against even
straightforward targets, let alone those designed to foil defenses. In April
of 1999, for the sixth time in a row, a high-altitude area-defense interceptor missile missed its target.[15]

Even more important, the United States has demonstrated that it will
not honor the 1972 Anti-Ballistic Missile Treaty that clearly prohibits a
national missile defense. Other countries have not missed this implication and have threatened to take appropriate actions. Russia has made it
clear that its implementation of the START agreements, which would result in the reduction of thousands of warheads from its arsenal, depends
on continued U.S. compliance with this treaty. China, too, is deeply opposed to a U.S. national missile defense system. While China has only
some two dozen long-range missiles now, it claims it will seek to upgrade
its nuclear arsenal if the United States develops and deploys such a missile defense system. Nevertheless, Secretary of Defense William Cohen
has said that the only remaining obstacle to deployment is "technological readiness."

Thus, instead of using the post–Cold War period to reduce the nuclear standoff and build a cooperative relationship with Russia and China,
the United States is undermining the basis of arms reductions.

Tritium production

There are other indications that reductions in nuclear arms are unlikely
to proceed at a fast rate. In December 1998, after considering various op-
tions to resume production of tritium, Secretary of Energy Bill Richardson
announced that the United States will use the Tennessee Valley Authority's Watts Bar Nuclear Plant to produce tritium when it is needed. He also
said that DOE will continue research on alternative means to produce tritium. Tritium, a radioactive gas with a relatively short half-life, is used to
increase the explosive power in nuclear weapons. The current U.S. stock-

pile is sufficient to supply 8,400 weapons with tritium until 2010.[16] This determination to increase production of tritium is further evidence that U.S. actions belie its position as stated in international agreements.

START II specifically calls for Russia and the United States to reduce their deployed strategic nuclear warheads to a maximum of 3,500 each. Moreover, at the 1996 Helsinki summit, presidents Clinton and Yeltsin agreed to reduce the numbers even further, to 2,500 each by December 2007. Russia has proposed cutting these numbers by yet another 1,000 each. With 2,500 or 1,500 strategic weapons and 1,000 tactical weapons, the United States would not need new tritium till 2025 or 2030. By deciding to resume tritium production instead of vigorously pursuing reductions, the United States has sent a signal to Russia and the international community that it seeks to maintain its current arsenal levels.

Towards abolition

As the United States tries to maintain and modernize its nuclear arsenal, most countries are becoming increasingly impatient with the nuclear weapons states for their failure to deliver on their promises of nuclear disarmament. This is nothing new. In fact, the very first resolution passed by the UN [United Nations] General Assembly at its founding in 1946 called for nuclear disarmament. Since then, there have been hundreds of resolutions calling for the same goal. What is new is the growing awareness that the traditional excuse given by the superpowers for maintaining their arsenals—that is, the threat to their security posed by their Cold War rivalry—is no longer valid.

One of the clearest commitments to nuclear disarmament made by the United States and the four other countries that had tested nuclear weapons before 1967 is in the 1970 Nuclear Non-Proliferation Treaty. Under Article VI of this treaty, the nuclear weapons states agreed to eliminate their nuclear weapons. In exchange, the other signatories to the treaty forswore their right to develop them.

U.S. policies actually have the perverse effect of strengthening arguments by other states in their quest for nuclear weapons.

It is worth emphasizing that the nonnuclear weapons states have, almost without exception, kept their end of the bargain while the nuclear weapons states have conducted innumerable nuclear weapons tests and increased the size and destructive power of their arsenals. The Natural Resources Defense Council estimates that in 1967 there were some 40,000 nuclear weapons in the world, and that this number increased to 69,000 in 1986, before falling back to around 36,000 in 1997.[17]

It is clear that the nonproliferation treaty was not in itself sufficient to prevent increases in nuclear arsenals. Only the end of the Cold War and the collapse of the Soviet Union accomplished that. However, despite the complete disappearance of any justification for these nuclear arsenals, the numbers of warheads maintained by the nuclear states today suggest that these nations do not intend to keep their side of the bargain and eliminate their nuclear arsenals any time in the near future. The present impasse and bleak future for disarmament have led to calls for a "peasants' revolt"—a mass withdrawal by nonnuclear weapons states from the treaty unless the nuclear weapons states "agree in some forum to start genuine negotiations designed to ultimately rid the world of nuclear weapons."[18] There have also been suggestions to amend the nuclear nonproliferation treaty so that it completely outlaws nuclear weapons.[19]

The intent of these negotiations is not to disarm the United States . . . the intent of U.S. arms negotiators is to disarm others.

It is also clear that the nuclear weapons states have a legal obligation to abolish nuclear weapons. In 1994, the United Nations General Assembly asked the International Court of Justice—the World Court—whether the threat or use of nuclear weapons in any circumstances would be permitted under international law. In response, the Court held that "the threat or use of nuclear weapons would generally be contrary to the rules of international law applicable in armed conflict, and in particular the principles and rules of humanitarian law." Further, the Court went on to state unanimously that "there exists an obligation to pursue in good faith and bring to a conclusion negotiations leading to nuclear disarmament in all its aspects under strict and effective international control."[20]

Recent initiatives

On November 6, 1996, Malaysia, along with 24 other sponsors, introduced an important resolution at the United Nations, calling for compliance with the World Court opinion and negotiations toward the abolition of nuclear weapons.[21] The resolution was adopted on December 10, 1996, with the support of 115 of the member states of the UN, with 22 votes against and 32 abstentions. Significantly, the nuclear weapons states, other than China, were opposed. Law, it seems, was not meant for them.

In a separate UN vote, 139 states supported the World Court's position on the obligation to negotiate nuclear disarmament. Similar resolutions were passed in 1997 and 1998. And in the latest round of voting at the UN, 123 states voted in support of the whole resolution, and 159 states voted in support of the paragraph underlining the World Court judgement.

In 1998, a coalition of countries—Ireland, South Africa, New Zealand, Sweden, Brazil, Egypt, and Mexico—presented a UN resolution intended "to galvanize the international community in common action for the purpose of eradicating [nuclear] weapons for once and for all." This resolution also aimed at challenging traditional thinking on nuclear policy and complacency among nuclear weapons states and suggested practical steps to move beyond the nuclear prison of 20th century policy.

Britain, France, and the United States launched a concerted effort to persuade their nuclear umbrella allies, North Atlantic Treaty Organization [NATO], and those countries of Eastern Europe that seek admission to the

European Union or NATO, to vote against the coalition resolution. Despite those efforts, several countries including 12 of the 16 NATO members abstained from voting, indicating their displeasure at current U.S. and NATO policies. Following the vote, the political debates in many countries over the UN resolution prompted Germany, Canada, and others to push harder for a reexamination of NATO strategies.[22] In particular, these countries want to seriously reappraise the traditional assumption that a policy of first use of nuclear weapons poses a significant deterrent to the initiation of war by other nations.

There has also been similar pressure for achieving disarmament from the Conference on Disarmament—the international body where nuclear arms control and disarmament treaties are traditionally negotiated. During the February 1999 session, five initiatives toward nuclear disarmament were submitted.[23]

Among them are proposals by South Africa—which unilaterally dismantled its nuclear program in the early 1990s and thereby earned respect as an important advocate of nuclear disarmament—and a joint proposal by five NATO member states: Belgium, Germany, Italy, the Netherlands, and Norway. This last proposal is particularly significant since it indicates a split within countries that have generally supported U.S. policy. Another NATO country, Canada, has also submitted a separate proposal calling for nuclear disarmament.

Recommendations

Over the last few years, there have been several recommendations from nongovernmental organizations, both within the United States and worldwide, for a systematic push for nuclear disarmament. One of the most ambitious of these proposals is a nuclear weapons convention. Modeled after the chemical and biological weapons conventions, this convention would prohibit the development, production, testing, deployment, stockpiling, transfer, threat, or use of nuclear weapons and would provide for their elimination. In 1997, Costa Rica introduced a model nuclear weapons convention at the United Nations, and the following year, U.S. Representative Lynn Woolsey introduced a resolution urging President Clinton to initiate multilateral negotiations leading to the early conclusion of such a convention.[24]

Most countries are becoming increasingly impatient with the nuclear weapons states for their failure to deliver on their promises of nuclear disarmament.

Several interim steps have also been advocated. For example, Professor Frank von Hippel, who served as assistant director for national security in the White House Office of Science and Technology Policy, and others have recommended that missiles be pulled off hair-trigger alert as a step towards deep reductions of nuclear arsenals.[25] Similarly, Admiral Stansfield Turner, a former director of the CIA, has made a case for strategic escrow—removing nuclear warheads from their delivery vehicles and placing them in separate, monitored, storage sites.[26]

Not all recommendations address the technicalities of delivery vehicles and warheads. Some have suggested changes at the operational and doctrinal level, including no-first-use commitments that guarantee no country would use nuclear weapons first in a conflict. Some NATO members have also sought to implement this as part of NATO strategy. Others prefer to go further and call for a commitment from nuclear weapons states to not use nuclear weapons under any circumstances.

Peace at last?

More than 30 years after the nuclear weapons states committed to nuclear disarmament, there are still no signs of any serious steps towards the widely shared goal of a nuclear-weapon-free world. Instead, by pointing to dubious threats, the United States seems to be expanding its abilities to maintain its nuclear arsenal at considerable cost. This only incites other countries to follow similar policies, increasing insecurity all around. In addition, several policies not directly related to nuclear weapons also affect this state of affairs. For example, the addition of new Eastern European members in NATO, and NATO's decision to bomb Serbia without going through the United Nations, have led to calls within Russia to increase its reliance on nuclear weapons. Similarly, the double standard with respect to countries of the Middle East also increases incentives for other countries to develop their own arsenals. Israel, for example, has developed a nuclear arsenal but continues to receive huge amounts of military aid from the United States, whereas Iraq has been punished with a murderous international regime of sanctions for its much smaller-scale nuclear pursuits.

The post–Cold War era has given us the gift of time to rid the world of nuclear dangers.[27] Russia is on the verge of economic collapse, and the other nuclear weapons states have much smaller nuclear arsenals than either Russia or the United States. Today, the only country capable of rapid strides towards nuclear abolition is the United States. More than 50 years ago, the United States took the lead in developing nuclear weapons; now it must take the lead in ridding the world of these weapons of mass destruction.

Notes

1. For the text of the treaty, see US Arms Control and Disarmament Agency, *Arms Control and Disarmament Agreements* (Washington, DC: US Arms Control and Disarmament Agency, 1990). Also available on the Internet at http://www.acda.gov.

2. Jaswant Singh, "Against Nuclear Apartheid," *Foreign Affairs* (September/October 1998).

3. "Remarks by the President on the Patients' Bill of Rights," Office of the Press Secretary, the White House, May 28, 1998.

4. Andrew Lichterman and Jacqueline Cabasso, *A Faustian Bargain: Why Stockpile Stewardship is Incompatible with the Process of Nuclear Disarmament* (Oakland, CA: Western States Legal Foundation, March 1998).

5. US Department of Energy, *Final Programmatic Environmental Impact State-*

ment for Stockpile Stewardship and Management (September 1996), p. S-3.

6. Peter Gray, *"Stockpile Stewardship" of Nuclear Weapons: The Deal to Subsidize Nuclear Weapons* (Santa Barbara, CA: Tides Foundation, Project for Participatory Democracy, March 1998).

7. Christopher E. Paine and Matthew G. McKinzie, *End Run: The U.S. Government's Plan for Designing Nuclear Weapons and Simulating Nuclear Explosions under the Comprehensive Test Ban Treaty* (Natural Resources Defense Council Report, August 1997).

8. William Broad, "U.S. Plan Shows New Design Work on Nuclear Weapons," *New York Times* (August 18, 1997), p. 1.

9. M.V. Ramana, "The Hawks Take Flight: India and the Fissile Material Cutoff," *International Network of Engineers and Scientists against Proliferation Bulletin,* 13 (July 1997); available on the Internet at http://www.th-darmstadt.de/ze/ianus/inesap/current.html.

10. R. Jeffrey Smith, "Clinton Directive Changes Strategy on Nuclear Weapons," *Washington Post* (December 7, 1997).

11. H.M. Kristensen, "Nuclear Futures: Proliferation of Weapons of Mass Destruction and U.S. Nuclear Strategy," BASIC Research Report 98.2 (London: British American Security Information Council,1998); available on the Internet at http://www.basicint.org/nfuture2.htm.

12. Robert S. Norris and William M. Arkin, "U.S. Nuclear Stockpile, July 1997," *Bulletin of the Atomic Scientists* (July/August 1997), pp. 66–67.

13. US Department of Energy, *Final Environmental Impact Statement for the Continued Operation of the Pantex Plant and Associated Storage of Nuclear Weapon Components* (November 1996), pp. 1-7–1-10.

14. Rear Admiral W. J. Holland Jr., "Nuclear Weapons in the Info Age: Who Needs 'em?" *US Naval Institute Proceedings* (January 1999), p. 47.

15. Robert Wall, "Thaad Misses Target Again; Telemetry Loss Hinders Analysis," *Aviation Week and Space Technology* (April 5, 1999), p. 62.

16. Charles Ferguson and Frank von Hippel, "U.S. Tritium Production Plan Lacks Strategic Rationale," *Defense News* 29 (December 7–13, 1998).

17. Robert Norris and William Arkin, "Global Nuclear Stockpiles, 1945–1997," *Bulletin of the Atomic Scientists* (November/December 1997), p. 67.

18. Frank Blackaby, "Time for a Peasants' Revolt," *Bulletin of the Atomic Scientists* (November/December 1997), p. 4.

19. Zia Mian and M.V. Ramana, "Disarmament Judo: Using the NPT to Make the Nuclear Weapons States Negotiate the Abolition of Nuclear Weapons," *Disarmament Diplomacy* 36 (April 1999).

20. John Burroughs, *The Legality of Threat or Use of Nuclear Weapons: A Guide to the Historic Opinion of the International Court of Justice* (Piscataway, NJ: Transaction Publishers, 1998).

21. UN General Assembly Resolution, A/Res/51/45M.

22. "Germany Raises No-First-Use Issue at NATO Meeting," *Arms Control Today* (November/December 1998), p. 24.

23. Rebecca Johnson, "Geneva Update No. 44: Frustration That the CD Isn't Working," *Disarmament Diplomacy* (February 1999), pp. 16–19.

24. US House of Representatives Resolution 106/82, "Resolution on Further-
    ing Complete Nuclear Disarmament," available on the Internet at http://
    www.napf.orgres_a2000_woolsey.html.

25. Frank von Hippel, "Paring Down the Arsenal," *Bulletin of the Atomic Sci-
    entists* (May/June 1997), pp. 33–40.

26. Stansfield Turner, *Caging the Nuclear Genie* (Boulder, CO: Westview Press,
    1997).

27. Jonathan Schell, *The Gift of Time: The Case for Abolishing Nuclear Weapons*
    (New York: Henry Holt & Company, 1998).

Organizations to Contact

The editors have compiled the following list of organizations concerned with the issues debated in this book. The descriptions are derived from materials provided by the organizations. All have publications or information available for interested readers. The list was compiled on the date of publication of the present volume; the information provided here may change. Be aware that many organizations take several weeks or longer to respond to inquiries, so allow as much time as possible.

The American Civil Defense Association (TACDA)
PO Box 1057, Starke, FL 32091
(800) 425-5397 • (904) 964-5397 • fax: (904) 964-9641
e-mail: defense@tacda.org • website: www.tacda.org

TACDA was established in the early 1960s in an effort to help promote civil defense awareness and disaster preparedness, both in the military and private sector, and to assist citizens in their efforts to prepare for all types of natural and man-made disasters. Publications include the quarterly *Journal of Civil Defense* and the *TACDA Alert* newsletter.

America's Future
7800 Bonhomme Ave., St. Louis, MO 63105
(314) 725-6003 • fax: (314) 721-3373
e-mail: info@americasfuture.net • website: www.americasfuture.net

America's Future seeks to educate the public about the importance of the principles upon which the U.S. government is founded and on the value of the free enterprise system. It supports continued U.S. testing of nuclear weapons and their usefulness as a deterrent of war. The group publishes the monthly newsletter *America's Future*.

Arms Control Association (ACA)
1726 M St. NW, Suite 201, Washington, DC 20036
(202) 463-8270 • fax: (202) 463-8273
e-mail: aca@armscontrol.org • website: www.armscontrol.org

The Arms Control Association is a nonprofit organization dedicated to promoting public understanding of and support for effective arms control policies. The ACA seeks to increase public appreciation of the need to limit arms, reduce international tensions, and promote world peace. It publishes the monthly magazine *Arms Control Today*.

Carnegie Endowment for International Peace
1779 Massachusetts Ave. NW, Washington, DC 20036
(202) 483-7600 • fax: (202) 483-1840
e-mail: info@ceip.org • website: www.ceip.org

The Carnegie Endowment for International Peace conducts research on international affairs and U.S. foreign policy. Issues concerning nuclear weapons

87

and proliferation are often discussed in articles published in its quarterly journal *Foreign Policy*.

Center for Defense Information (CDI)
1779 Massachusetts Ave. NW, Suite 615, Washington, DC 20036
(202) 332-0600 • fax: (202) 462-4559
e-mail: info@cdi.org • website: www.cdi.org

The CDI comprises civilians and former military officers who oppose both excessive expenditures for weapons and policies that increase the danger of war. The center serves as an independent monitor of the military, analyzing spending, policies, weapon systems, and related military issues. It publishes the *Defense Monitor* ten times per year.

Center for Nonproliferation Studies
Monterey Institute for International Studies
425 Van Buren St., Monterey, CA 93940
(831) 647-4154 • fax: (831) 647-3519
website: http://cns.miis.edu

The center researches all aspects of nonproliferation and works to combat the spread of weapons of mass destruction. The center produces research databases and has multiple reports, papers, speeches, and congressional testimony available online. Its main publication is *The Nonproliferation Review*, which is published three times per year.

Henry L. Stimson Center
11 Dupont Circle NW, 9th Floor, Washington, DC 20036
(202) 223-5956 • fax: (202) 238-9604
website: www.stimson.org

The Stimson Center is an independent, nonprofit public policy institute committed to finding and promoting innovative solutions to the security challenges confronting the United States and other nations. The center directs the Chemical and Biological Weapons Nonproliferation Project, which serves as a clearinghouse of information related to the monitoring and implementation of the 1993 Chemical Weapons Convention. The center produces occasional papers, reports, handbooks, and books on chemical and biological weapon policy, nuclear policy, and eliminating weapons of mass destruction.

Peace Action
1819 H St. NW, Suite 425, Washington, DC 20006
(202) 862-9740 • fax: (202) 862-9762
e-mail: paprog@igc.org • website: www.peace-action.org

Peace Action is a grassroots peace and justice organization that works for policy changes in Congress and the United Nations, as well as state and city legislatures. The national office houses an organizing department that promotes education and activism on topics related to peace and disarmament issues. The organization produces a quarterly newsletter and also publishes an annual voting record for members of Congress.

Project Ploughshares
Institute of Peace and Conflict Studies, Conrad Grebel College
Waterloo, ON N2L 3G6 Canada
(519) 888-6541 fax: (519) 885-0806
e-mail: plough@ploughshares.ca • website: www.ploughshares.ca

Project Ploughshares promotes disarmament and demilitarization, the peaceful resolution of political conflict, and the pursuit of security based on equity, justice, and a sustainable environment. Public understanding and support for these goals is encouraged through research, education, and development of constructive policy alternatives.

Union of Concerned Scientists (UCS)
2 Brattle Sq., Cambridge, MA 02238
(617) 547-5552 • fax: (617) 864-9405
e-mail: ucs@ucsusa.org • website: www.ucsusa.org

UCS is concerned about the impact of advanced technology on society. It supports nuclear arms control as a means to reduce nuclear weapons. Publications include the quarterly *Nucleus* newsletter and reports and briefs concerning nuclear proliferation.

United States Arms Control and Disarmament Agency (ACDA)
320 21st St. NW, Washington, DC 20451
(800) 581-ACDA • fax: (202) 647-6928
website: www.acda.gov

The mission of the agency is to strengthen the national security of the United States by formulating, advocating, negotiating, implementing, and verifying effective arms control, nonproliferation, and disarmament policies, strategies, and agreements. In doing so, ACDA ensures that arms control is fully integrated into the development and conduct of U.S. national security policy. The agency publishes fact sheets on the disarmament of weapons of mass destruction as well as online records of speeches, treaties, and reports related to arms control.

Washington File
U.S. Information Agency
301 Fourth St. SW, Room 602, Washington, DC 20547
(202) 619-4355
e-mail: inquiry@usia.gov
website: www.usia.gov/products/washfile.htm

This website is a comprehensive source of current releases and government information relating to foreign affairs. It is maintained by the U.S. Information Agency, an independent foreign affairs agency within the executive branch of the U.S. government.

Bibliography

Books

Eric Arnett, ed. — *Implementing the Comprehensive Test Ban: New Aspects Of Definition, Organization, and Verification.* New York: Oxford University Press, 1996.

Eric Arnett, ed. — *Nuclear Weapons After the Comprehensive Test Ban: Implications for Modernization and Proliferation.* New York: Oxford University Press, 1996.

Lisa A. Baglione — *To Agree or Not to Agree: Leadership, Bargaining, and Arms Control.* Ann Arbor, MI: University of Michigan Press, 1999.

Harold A. Feiveson and Bruce G. Blair, eds. — *The Nuclear Turning Point: A Blueprint for Deep Cuts and De-Alerting of Nuclear Weapons.* Washington, DC: Brookings Institute, 1999.

James L. Ford — *Nuclear Smuggling: How Serious a Threat?* Washington, DC: National Defense University Press, 1996.

Lewis Gaddis, ed. — *Cold War Statesmen Confront the Bomb: Nuclear Diplomacy Since 1945.* New York: Oxford University Press, 1999.

Thomas E. Halverson — *The Last Great Nuclear Debate: NATO and Short-Range Nuclear Weapons in the 1980's.* New York: St. Martin's, 1995.

Douglas Holdstock and Frank Barnaby, eds. — *Hiroshima and Nagasaki Retrospect and Prospect.* London and Portland: Frank Cass, 1995.

Richard Kokoski — *Technology and the Proliferation of Nuclear Weapons.* New York: Oxford University Press, 1995.

David A. Koplow — *Testing a Nuclear Test Ban: What Should Be Prohibited by a "Comprehensive" Treaty?* Brookfield, VT: Dartmouth, 1996.

Arjun Makhijani, Howard Hu, and Katherine Yih — *Nuclear Wastelands: A Global Guide to Nuclear Weapons Production and Its Health and Environmental Effects.* Boston: MIT Press, 1995.

Keith B. Payne — *Deterrence in the Second Nuclear Age.* Lexington: University Press of Kentucky, 1997.

Mitchell Reiss — *Bridled Ambition: Why Countries Constrain Their Nuclear Capabilities.* Washington, DC: Woodrow Wilson Center Press, 1995.

Scott D. Sagan and Kenneth N. Waltz, eds. — *The Spread of Nuclear Weapons: A Debate.* New York: W.W. Norton, 1995.

Tom Sauer — *Nuclear Arms Control: Nuclear Deterrence in the Post–Cold War Period.* New York: St. Martin's, 1998.

Periodicals

Madeleine Albright	"The Spread of Nuclear Arms: The Necessity of Treaties," *Vital Speeches of the Day*, June 10, 1998.
William M. Arkin	"The Bomb Has Many Friends," *Bulletin of the Atomic Scientists*, March/April 1997.
Kathleen Bailey	"Why We Have to Keep the Bomb," *Bulletin of Atomic Scientists*, January/February 1995.
Tom Bethell	"No Nukes America," *American Spectator*, December 1996.
Richard K. Betts	"The New Threat of Mass Destruction," *Foreign Affairs*, January/February 1998.
Bruce Blair, Harold Feiveson, and Fran von Hippel	"Taking Nuclear Weapons off Hair-Trigger Alert," *Scientific American*, November 1997.
Ashton B. Carter and John M. Deutch	"No Nukes? Not Yet," *Wall Street Journal*, March 4, 1997.
Sam Cohen	"Save the Nukes," *National Review*, February 10, 1997.
Jonathan Dean and Randall Forsberg	"The Road to Zero," *Technology Review*, August/September 1995.
William Epstein	"Indefinite Extension—with Increased Accountability," *Bulletin of the Atomic Scientists*, July/August 1995.
Lisbeth Gronlund and David Wright	"Missile Defense: The Sequel," *Technology Review*, May/June 1997.
David Hughes	"When Terrorists Go Nuclear," *Popular Mechanics*, January 1996.
Melanie Kirkpatrick	"What's Blocking Missile Defense? A Defunct Treaty," *Wall Street Journal*, August 3, 1998.
Andrew F. Krepinevich Jr.	"Forging a Path to a Post-Nuclear U.S. Military," *Issues in Science and Technology*, Spring 1997.
William C. Martel	"Puncturing the 'Loose Nukes' Myth," *USA Today*, March 1997.
Johanna McGeary	"The Whites of His Eyes," *Time*, November 23, 1998.
Greg Mello, Andrew Lichterman, and William Weida	"The Stockpile Stewardship Charade," *Issues in Science and Technology*, Spring 1999.
Bruce W. Nelan	"Nuclear Disarray," *Time*, May 19, 1997.
Douglas Pasternak	"American Colleges Are 'Weapons U.' for Iraq," *U.S. News & World Report*, March 9, 1998.
William Pfaff	"Nuclear Deterrence," *Commonweal*, October 8, 1999.
James Schlesinger	"Nukes: Test Them or Lose Them," *Wall Street Journal*, November 19, 1997.
Stephen I. Schwartz	"Four Trillion Dollars and Counting," *Bulletin of the Atomic Scientists*, November/December 1995.
Jaswant Singh	"Against Nuclear Apartheid," *Foreign Affairs*, September/October 1998.
Henry Sokolski	"A Blast of Reality," *New York Times*, May 13, 1998.

Index